Les Misérables

VICTOR HUGO
Translated by Norman Denny

Level 6

Retold by Chris Rice
Series Editors: Andy Hopkins and Jocelyn Potter

Pearson Education Limited
Edinburgh Gate, Harlow,
Essex CM20 2JE, England
and Associated Companies throughout the world.

ISBN 0 582 50508 9

First published 1862
This translation first published by the Folio Press 1976
This edition first published by Penguin Books 2002

3 5 7 9 10 8 6 4 2

Typeset by Ferdinand Pageworks, London
Set in 11/14pt Bembo
Reproduction by Spectrum Colour, Ipswich
Printed in Spain by Mateu Cromo, S.A. Pinto (Madrid)

Published by Pearson Education Limited in association with
Penguin Books Ltd, both companies being subsidiaries of Pearson Plc

Contents

		page
Introduction		v
Chapter 1	Jean Valjean	1
Chapter 2	Fantine	10
Chapter 3	Monsieur Madeleine	14
Chapter 4	The Man in the Long Yellow Coat	22
Chapter 5	Valjean and Cosette	27
Chapter 6	Marius	31
Chapter 7	The Jondrettes	38
Chapter 8	Marius and Cosette	52
Chapter 9	Monsieur Gillenormand	58
Chapter 10	The Barricade	62
Chapter 11	The Letter	69
Chapter 12	Fight to the Death	72
Chapter 13	The Sewers of Paris	76
Chapter 14	The Wedding	83
Chapter 15	The Truth at Last	88
Activities		99

Introduction

'When will the meal be ready?' the stranger asked.

'I'm sorry, Monsieur,' the innkeeper said. 'You can't stay here. I've got no free rooms.'

'Then put me in a stable. All I need is a quiet corner somewhere.'

The innkeeper approached and, bending towards the man, said in a fierce whisper, 'Get out. I know who you are. Your name is Jean Valjean. You've just been released from prison. I can't serve people like you here.'

After spending nineteen years in prison for stealing a loaf of bread, Jean Valjean is at last a free man. But he is a cold, tired, hungry man, with no money and not a friend in the world. Entering the small town of Digne, he looks for food and shelter for the night, but without success. He is rejected and insulted by everyone he meets. Angry and bitter at the cruel injustice of life, he settles down to spend the night on a stone bench in the town square. But then something happens that will change his life forever. He discovers love, and spends the rest of his life trying to help people, like himself, who have been unfortunate victims of poverty and social injustice – 'les misérables'.

As we join Valjean on his journey through life, we meet many unforgettable characters: Javert, the cold-hearted police inspector, whose aim in life is to send Valjean back to prison; the evil Thénardiers; the tragic mother, Fantine, and her beautiful daughter, Cosette; the penniless but noble young man, Marius. Although Valjean does his best to help the unhappy people he meets, he finds that he is unable to escape from the ghosts of his own terrible past. He meets danger everywhere. Will the love that burns in Valjean's heart survive the misery of a cruel and unjust world? Or will he be defeated and destroyed by enemies who cannot understand goodness?

Victor Hugo's *Les Misérables* is one of the greatest novels of the nineteenth century. In the book, he describes and criticizes the social injustice in France between the fall of Napoleon in 1815 and the failed revolution against King Louis-Philippe in 1832. He writes in his own introduction to the book: 'The laws and customs of France create a social condition which is a kind of human hell. As long as unawareness and poverty exist on Earth, books such as this will always be needed.'

'Les Misérables' is a French phrase that cannot be translated exactly into English. In French, it has two meanings. It means 'people who live in misery'; it also means, 'people who live outside society in total poverty'. Hugo's interest in social justice and his concern for these 'misérables' is obvious. But it is not Hugo's desire to improve conditions for the ordinary citizens of France that make this a great novel. *Les Misérables* is a great novel because Hugo was a Romantic★ at heart, and the book is filled with moments of great poetry and beauty. It has a depth of vision and inner truth that make it a timeless classic, one of the great works of western literature. Even today, 150 years after it was written, *Les Misérables* is a powerful story. It has been made into many films and plays. In 1986, a musical version opened in London. It was an enormous success, and is still extremely popular in theatres in London, New York and other cities around the world.

Born in Besançon, France, in 1802, Victor-Marie Hugo decided at an early age to be a writer. In 1817, aged fifteen, he was honoured by a literary organization for a poem, and he published his first book of poems when he was twenty. Over the next sixty years, he wrote twenty books of poetry, nine novels and ten plays, and produced a huge amount of literary, political and other writing. His

★ Romantics: in the early nineteenth century, many writers and artists believed in the importance of individual feelings, the power of freedom and the beauty of language and dreams.

best years were 1829–43. His great historical novel, *The Hunchback of Notre Dame* (1831) made him popular. He wrote several successful books of poetry. He also wrote plays, two of which – *Hernani* (1830) and *The King Amuses Himself* (1832) – were adapted by Verdi for his operas *Ernani* (1844) and *Rigoletto* (1851).

However, 1843 was a bad year for Hugo. His play, *The Governors*, was a failure. But then something much more serious happened, which affected him badly for a long time: his eldest daughter and her husband drowned in an accident. For many years, Hugo stopped writing fiction and concentrated on politics. As a young man, Hugo had supported the Royal Family, despite his parents' support for the republic of Napoleon. In later years, however, although he received many honours from King Louis-Philippe, he became more republican himself. At first, he was happy when Louis-Philippe was forced from power in 1848 and Louis Napoleon became President of a newly-formed republic. But Hugo soon realized that he disliked Louis Napoleon (later Napoleon III). He criticized him openly, and in 1851 he was forced to leave the country. He lived with his wife and family for fourteen years on the British island of Guernsey, where, among other things, he wrote *Les Misérables* (1862).

Hugo returned to France after the defeat of Napoleon III in the Franco-Prussian War in 1870. He was welcomed back as a national hero, and he achieved very high positions in the government. When he died in 1885, the whole country was filled with grief. Hugo, however, had always said that he did not want a large, expensive funeral. According to his wishes, his body was carried in a poor man's coffin and buried in the Panthéon, where many famous French citizens were buried.

Victor Hugo will always be remembered as one of the world's greatest and most important writers. He is still considered one of the finest French poets who ever lived. The power and beauty of his greatest novel, *Les Misérables*, will probably last forever.

Chapter 1   Jean Valjean

One evening in October 1815, an hour before sunset, a man with a long beard and dusty, torn clothes walked into the town of Digne. He was in his late forties, of medium height, broad-shouldered and strong. A leather cap half-hid his face, which was sunburnt and shining with sweat. His rough yellow shirt was unbuttoned, revealing a hairy chest. On his back was a heavy soldier's bag, and in his hand was a large wooden stick.

The townspeople, who had never seen him before, watched with interest as he stopped for water at a fountain. Children followed him to the marketplace, where he stopped for more water at another fountain. He then crossed the square towards an inn, and entered by the kitchen door.

The innkeeper, who was also the cook, was busy with his pots and pans, preparing a meal for a group of travellers who were laughing and joking in the next room.

'What can I do for you, Monsieur?'* he asked without looking up.

'A meal and a bed,' said the stranger.

'Of course.' The innkeeper turned to look at him. Then, seeing the visitor's rough appearance, he added, 'If you can pay for it.'

'I have money.' The stranger produced an old leather purse from his jacket.

'Then you're welcome,' the innkeeper said.

The stranger smiled with relief and sat down by the fire. He did not see a young boy run out with a note that the innkeeper had quickly written. He did not see the boy return a short time later and whisper something to the innkeeper.

'When will the meal be ready?' the stranger asked.

* Monsieur, Madame, Mademoiselle: the French words for Mr/Sir, Mrs/Madam and Miss. The short forms are M., Mme and Mlle.

'I'm sorry, Monsieur,' the innkeeper said. 'You can't stay here. I've got no free rooms.'

'Then put me in a stable. All I need is a quiet corner somewhere. After dinner . . .'

'You can't eat here either,' the innkeeper interrupted. 'I haven't enough food.'

'What about all that food in the pots?'

The innkeeper approached and, bending towards the man, said in a fierce whisper, 'Get out. I know who you are. Your name is Jean Valjean. You've just been released from prison. I can't serve people like you here.'

The man rose without another word, picked up his bag and stick, and left. Outside, it was growing dark and a cold wind was blowing from the mountains in the east. The man looked around, desperate for somewhere to spend the night. He tried another inn, but the same thing happened. He knocked on the doors of people's houses, but news of his arrival had quickly spread and nobody would offer him shelter from the cold. He even tried sleeping in a garden, but was chased away by a dog. Finally, he found himself in the cathedral square. He shook his fist at the church and then, cold and hungry, he lay down on a stone bench by the doorway.

A few minutes later, an old woman came out of the cathedral and saw him lying there.

'What are you doing?' she asked.

He answered angrily, 'Can't you see? I'm trying to sleep.'

'On this bench, in this cold wind?'

'I've slept for nineteen years on a piece of wood. Now it's stone. What's the difference?'

'Why don't you go to an inn?'

'Because I haven't any money,' he lied.

The old woman opened her purse and gave him a few coins. Then she said, 'Have you tried everywhere?'

'I've knocked at every door.'

'What about that one over there?' she said, pointing across the square to a small house beside the bishop's palace.

◆

The Bishop of Digne was a kind old man who, many years earlier, had given his palace to the town hospital. He lived a simple life with his sister, Mademoiselle Baptistine, and his old servant, Madame Magloire, and he was much loved by the people in the town. He trusted everyone. His doors were never locked, so that anybody who needed his help could find him easily.

That evening, Mme Magloire was chatting with Mlle Baptistine before serving the meal.

'People say there's a stranger in town,' she said. 'The police say that he looks dangerous, and it would be better for everyone to lock their windows and doors.'

'Brother.' Mlle Baptistine turned to the bishop, who was sitting by the fire. 'Did you hear what Mme Magloire was saying?'

'Something about a dangerous stranger walking the streets?' he asked with an amused smile.

'This is no joke,' Mme Magloire said. 'The man is in rags and has an evil look on his face. Everybody in the town agrees that something terrible will happen tonight. And your sister agrees with me that this house isn't safe. If you like, I can make arrangements now to get a lock put on the door ...'

Before the bishop could reply, there was a heavy knock on the door.

'Come in,' said the bishop.

The door opened and Jean Valjean, the stranger, walked in. Mme Magloire trembled, open-mouthed with fear, while Mlle Baptistine rose from her seat with alarm. The bishop, however, looked calmly at his unexpected visitor.

'My name is Jean Valjean,' the stranger said before anybody could speak. 'I've been in prison for nineteen years. They let me out four days ago. I've been walking all day, and nobody in this town will give me food or a bed for the night. A woman saw me lying on a stone bench across the square and suggested that I come here. So here I am. What is this place? Is it an inn? I've got money. Will you let me stay?'

'Mme Magloire,' said the bishop, 'will you please prepare another place at the table for this gentleman?'

Valjean took a step forward. 'No, you don't understand,' he said. 'I've spent five years in prison for violent robbery, another fourteen years for trying to escape four times. I'm a dangerous man.'

'Mme Magloire,' the bishop went on, 'you must put clean sheets on the bed in the spare room.'

Mme Magloire, an obedient servant, left the room without protest.

The bishop turned to the man. 'Sit down and warm yourself, Monsieur. Supper will soon be ready.'

Jean Valjean's face, which had been hard and fierce, suddenly softened. 'You really mean it?' he asked, his voice trembling with childish excitement. 'You'll let me stay? I'm a dangerous criminal, but you called me "Monsieur". I don't believe it. May I ask your name, sir? Are you an innkeeper?'

'I'm a priest,' said the bishop. 'And this is where I live.'

'A priest?' Valjean said, sitting by the fire. 'So I don't have to pay?'

'You can keep your money,' the bishop replied.

During dinner, Mlle Baptistine looked at Valjean kindly while the bishop talked about the local cheese-making industry. Valjean was so hungry that, at first, he paid no attention to anyone. Soon, however, he began to relax, and looked around the room. 'This is not the house of a rich man,' he thought. 'And the travellers in the inn eat better than this.' But then he looked at the table, and saw the beautiful silver candlesticks, knives and forks.

After dinner, the bishop said goodnight to his sister, picked up one of the two candlesticks and, handing the other to his guest, said, 'I'll show you to your room, Monsieur.'

Valjean followed the bishop upstairs into a bedroom. This was the bishop's bedroom. As he was following the bishop across the room, however, he noticed Mme Magloire putting the silver knives and forks in a cupboard by the bed.

The bishop showed his guest into the spare room.

'Sleep well,' he said. 'Before you leave tomorrow, you must have a bowl of warm milk from our cows.'

Valjean was so tired that he fell asleep, fully-dressed, on top of the sheets, but he didn't sleep for long. When he woke up, the cathedral clock was striking two, but he had not woken because of this. He had woken because the bed was too comfortable; he had not slept in a proper bed for twenty years. Unable to return to sleep, he gazed into the darkness, thinking about the past twenty years. Life had been unjust to him, and he was angry. In 1795, he had lost his job as a tree-cutter. At that time he was looking after his sister, whose husband had died, and her seven children. Out of work, and with no food in the house, he had been arrested for trying to steal a loaf of bread. Now, at last, he was free, but he felt bitter and angry about his lost years. The world had been unfair to him, and he wanted revenge. Then, remembering the silver on the bishop's table, he had an idea.

He sat up, swung his feet to the floor and slowly stood up. The house was silent. He moved carefully towards the window and looked out. The night was not very dark; there was a full moon, hidden from time to time by large clouds moving quickly across the sky. After studying the garden, he decided that escape would be easy. He turned back to the room, picked up his bag and took out a short iron bar, sharpened at one end. He then put his shoes into the bag and, grasping the iron bar in his right hand, he moved quietly towards the door of the bishop's bedroom. It was half-open. The bishop had not closed it.

Valjean stood listening. There was no sound.

He gave the door a gentle push and crept into the bedroom. Just as he reached the side of the bishop's bed, the moon came out from behind a cloud and filled the room with light. Valjean gazed down at the bishop's gentle, sleeping face, and felt a kind of terror. He had never before seen such peace, such kindness, such trust.

He suddenly turned away and moved quickly to the cupboard. The first thing he saw when he opened the door was the basket of silver. He grabbed it, hurried back to the spare bedroom, picked up his stick and bag, climbed out of the window, emptied the silver into his bag and threw the basket into the garden. A minute later he climbed the garden wall and disappeared into the trees.

Early the next morning, while the bishop was studying the flowers in his garden, Mme Magloire ran out of the house with a look of alarm on her face.

'Monseigneur,* do you know where the silver-basket is?'

'Yes,' said the bishop. 'I found it in one of the flowerbeds.'

'But it's empty!' she cried. 'Where's the silver?'

'Oh, you're worried about the silver? I don't know where *that* is.'

'Heaven save us, it's been stolen!' she cried. 'The man who came last night! He's run off with our silver!'

The bishop, who had been bending sadly over a plant damaged by the basket, looked up and said gently, 'I think I was wrong to keep the silver for so long. It really belongs to the poor. I should have given it away a long time ago.'

---

* Monseigneur: a title given to people with a high position in the Church.

Later that morning, as the bishop and his sister were having breakfast, there was a knock on the door. Four men walked into the room. Three of them were policemen; the fourth was Jean Valjean.

'Monseigneur . . .' the sergeant in charge of the group began.

Valjean raised his head with surprise. 'Monseigneur?' he repeated. 'I thought he was a priest.'

'Silence,' said one of the policemen. 'This is the Bishop of Digne.'

The bishop, meanwhile, had moved towards the group of men and was smiling at Jean Valjean.

'I'm delighted to see you again, dear friend,' he said. 'But what about the candlesticks? I gave you those as well, don't you remember? They're silver like the rest, and worth at least two hundred francs. Did you forget to take them?'

Jean Valjean's eyes widened with disbelief.

'Monseigneur,' said the sergeant, 'do I understand that this man was telling the truth? We found this silver in his bag, and . . .'

'And he told you,' the bishop finished the sentence for him, 'that an old priest had given it to him? Yes, he was telling the truth.'

'So this man isn't a thief?' The sergeant looked as surprised as Valjean.

'Not at all. So you can let him go at once.'

The policemen let go of Valjean's arms. He moved his feet nervously, uncertain of what to say at first. Then he murmured, 'Am I really free to go?'

'Of course,' said the bishop. 'But this time, you mustn't forget your candlesticks.'

He fetched them from a shelf and gave them to Valjean.

'Now, go in peace,' he said softly.

The policemen left, but Valjean did not move. He did not know what to think. The bishop walked up to him and said in a low voice, 'Don't forget that you've promised to use the money to make yourself an honest man.'

Valjean, who did not remember having made such a promise, was silent.

'Jean Valjean,' the bishop continued, 'I've bought your soul from the Devil, and have given it to God.'

♦

Jean Valjean left the town and ran into the countryside, blindly following lanes and paths, not realizing that he was running in circles. He was filled with a strange kind of anger, but he did not know why. Finally, as evening fell, he sat on the ground, exhausted, and gazed across the fields at the distant mountains, wishing that he was back in prison. When he had been angry at the world, he had felt calm and sure of himself. But now, for the first time in twenty years, a man had shown him great kindness, and he did not know what to feel.

Suddenly, he heard the sound of singing. A boy of about ten years old was coming along a footpath with a small box on his back and dirty knees showing through holes in his trousers. As he sang, he threw a coin into the air and caught it before it fell. Not noticing Jean Valjean sitting by the side of the path, he threw the coin higher into the air. This time, however, he did not catch it and it rolled along the ground towards Valjean, who immediately put his foot on it.

The boy, unafraid, walked up to Valjean.

'Please, Monsieur, may I have my coin?'

'What's your name?' asked Valjean.

'Petit-Gervais,' said the boy, smiling trustfully. 'I'm a chimney sweep, and that money is all I have.'

'Go away,' said Valjean.

'Please, Monsieur, that's my money.'

Valjean lowered his head and did not reply.

'My money!' the boy cried. 'My piece of silver! My coin!'

Valjean seemed not to hear him. The boy seized his collar and shook him. 'I want my money!' he cried.

Valjean slowly raised his head and stared with a sort of amazement at the child. Then, reaching for his stick, he said, 'Go to Hell!'

The boy, suddenly afraid of the mad, fierce look in Valjean's eyes, turned and ran.

Valjean stood for some time gazing emptily around him at the sunset and the shadows moving in on him. Suddenly he shivered, as if he had become aware for the first time of the icy wind. He bent down to pick up his bag but, as he did so, he caught sight of the silver coin, half-buried by his foot in the earth.

It affected him like an electric shock. 'What's that?' he murmured. He stared at the coin with a look of puzzlement, as if he were trying to remember something. Then, with a sudden movement, he bent down and picked it up. He looked around but could see nothing in the darkness – just a purple mist rising slowly from the fields.

He called the boy's name, but there was no reply. Within minutes he was running along the path, shouting. 'Petit-Gervais! Petit-Gervais!' There was still no reply.

A short time later, he met a priest on horseback.

'Have you seen a boy go by?' he asked.

The priest shook his head. 'No. Why do you ask?'

Valjean produced two five-franc pieces and gave them to the priest. 'This is for your poor, Monsieur. He was a boy of about ten, a chimney sweep. Monsieur, you must report me to the police. I'm a thief. I stole money from him. Here, let me give you more money . . .'

But before Valjean could produce more coins, the priest rode away in terror.

Valjean looked for the boy for another hour, running along

the path, calling out his name, but with no success. Finally he stopped and sat, exhausted, on a rock. Then, his heart full of grief for what he had done, he buried his face in his hands and, for the first time in nineteen years, he cried.

Chapter 2   Fantine

On a spring evening in 1818, in the village of Montfermeil, not far from Paris, two little girls were playing on a swing outside a small inn. Their mother − a big, red-haired woman with a plain face − sat on the doorstep of the inn, watching them.

'You have two very pretty children, Madame,' a voice said from close beside her.

The woman looked round and saw a young woman with a child sleeping peacefully in her arms. The mother was young and pretty, but she looked poor and unhappy. She did not smile, and lines of sadness ran down the side of her pale cheeks. Her clothes were old and dirty, and she wore a tight, plain cap over her beautiful blonde hair.

'Thank you,' said the woman. 'Why don't you sit down for a minute? You look tired.' When the young woman had sat down next to her, the red-haired woman introduced herself. 'My name's Thénardier. My husband and I manage this inn.'

'My name's Fantine,' the young woman said. 'I used to work in Paris, but my husband died and I lost my job.' She could not tell Mme Thénardier the truth, which was that she had been made pregnant by a young man who had then abandoned her. 'I left Paris this morning to look for work in Montreuil,' she continued. 'My little girl walked some of the way, but she's very small. I had to carry her and she's fallen asleep.' As she spoke these words, she gave her daughter a loving kiss, which woke her up. The child's eyes were as wide and blue as her mother's. With a little laugh, she jumped off her mother's lap and ran to play with the two girls on the swing.

'What's your little girl's name?' Mme Thénardier asked.

'Euphrasie – but I call her Cosette. She's nearly three.'

The two women watched the children playing together.

'Children make friends very easily, don't they?' Mme Thénardier smiled. 'Look at them. They could easily be sisters.'

At these words, Fantine did a very strange thing. She took Mme Thénardier's hand and said, 'Will you look after my daughter for me?'

Mme Thénardier looked at Fantine thoughtfully, but said nothing.

'I can't take her with me,' Fantine continued. 'I have to find work, and that's not easy with a child but no husband. As soon as I find a job, I'll come and fetch her. Will you do that for me? I could pay six francs a month.'

Mme Thénardier still said nothing, but a man's voice from inside the house called, 'We'll take seven francs a month, and six months in advance.'

Fantine agreed.

'And another fifteen francs for extras,' called the man.

'You will have them,' said Fantine, assuming that she was talking to Mme Thénardier's husband. 'I have eighty francs.'

'Does the child have enough clothes?' the man asked.

'She has some beautiful clothes,' Fantine replied. 'Plenty of everything and silk dresses like a lady. They're all in my bag.'

The man's face finally appeared in the doorway.

'Then we agree to look after her for you,' he said.

The next morning, Fantine kissed her daughter goodbye and left for Montreuil, crying as if her heart would break.

'This money will be useful,' Thénardier said to his wife. 'Now I can pay off all my debts and stay out of prison. I'm proud of you. You set a very clever trap.'

11

'Without even intending to,' his wife replied.

One month later, Thénardier was short of money again, so he took Cosette's beautiful silk clothes to Paris and sold them for sixty francs. The couple dressed Cosette in rags and gave her very little food, which they made her eat from a wooden bowl under the table. The dog and the cat, who ate with her, were her only companions.

Fantine, meanwhile, found work in Montreuil and asked for news of her daughter every month. The Thénardiers always replied that she was in good health and very happy. At the end of the year, however, Thénardier was not happy with just seven francs a month; he demanded twelve and Fantine paid without protest, happy that her daughter was being well cared for.

The Thénardiers, who were loving and gentle to their own daughters, Éponine and Azelma, treated Cosette like a slave.

They made her get up before dawn every day and do all the dirty jobs around the house, while Éponine and Azelma wore pretty clothes and played with dolls. By the age of five, Cosette had become a thin, pale-faced, silent child. Misery had made her ugly and only her beautiful blue eyes remained.

The Thénardiers did not feel guilty about treating Cosette badly because Fantine had stopped sending them regular payments.

'The child is lucky to have a home at all,' they told everybody. 'Without us, she'd be living on the streets.'

◆

When Fantine first arrived in Montreuil, she had immediately found work in a factory. She rented a small room, sent money regularly to the Thénardiers and, for a short time, was almost happy. She forgot many of her problems, and dreamt only of Cosette and her plans for the future. But her happiness did not last long. Although she was careful to say nothing about her daughter to anyone, other women at the factory soon discovered her secret. An unmarried woman with a child was a terrible thing in those days, and Fantine lost her job. She tried to find work as a servant, but no one would employ her. She finally managed to earn a little money sewing shirts, but she was unable to send money regularly to the Thénardiers.

That winter, Fantine saved money by not having a fire, and developed a small, dry cough. By the following winter, her debts had increased. The Thénardiers wrote her a frightening letter in which they told her that Cosette had no clothes, and that they needed ten francs immediately to buy her a new dress. Fantine, who did not have ten francs, but who was afraid that her daughter would freeze to death, went to the barber's shop. She took out her comb and let her blonde hair fall down to her waist.

'Such beautiful hair!' the barber said.

'How much will you give me for it?' Fantine asked.

'Ten francs.'

'Then cut it off.'

After selling her hair to the barber, Fantine was able to buy a woollen dress, which she sent to the Thénardiers. The Thénardiers, however, were very angry – they had wanted money, not clothes. They gave the dress to their daughter, Éponine, and Cosette went on shivering.

A few weeks later, Fantine received another letter from the Thénardiers. This time they wanted forty francs because Cosette was very ill and urgently needed medicine. Fantine felt desperate; she did not know how to obtain such a large sum of money. As she was wandering around the town, desperately trying to decide what to do, she noticed a crowd of people in the market square. She approached them without thinking, and discovered that they had gathered around a travelling dentist. Forgetting her troubles for a moment, she smiled at the dentist's humorous efforts to sell the people of Montreuil false teeth.

Suddenly the dentist saw her.

'You've got lovely teeth,' he said. 'If you sold me your two front teeth, I'd pay you forty francs.'

Fantine ran home, upset and disgusted. 'My hair will grow again,' she thought, 'but teeth would be gone forever.' But then she thought about her daughter, and her own appearance suddenly seemed unimportant. That evening, she visited the dentist at the inn where he was staying, and allowed him to remove her teeth.

Fantine could not sleep that night. She sat on her bed, cold and shivering, and looked at the two coins shining on the table. Then she gave a blood-stained smile. 'I'm happy,' she told herself. 'My baby isn't going to die.'

Fantine earned less and less money from her sewing, and the Thénardiers demanded more and more money to look after Cosette. Fantine spent whole nights crying. What could she do? She had sold her hair and her teeth; what else could she sell? And then she decided that she had no other choice: she would have to sell herself.

She became a prostitute.

Chapter 3   Monsieur Madeleine

One winter's evening, a toothless woman with a grey face and flowers in her hair was arrested for attacking a man in the street. She was taken to the police station, where Inspector Javert, the chief of police, sent her to prison for six months.

'Please, M. Javert.' The woman fell to her knees. 'I owe a hundred francs. If I don't pay, my little girl will lose her home and be thrown out on to the streets. Please don't send me to prison.'

Javert listened to her coldly, then ordered a policeman to take her away. While the policeman was trying to drag her to her feet, however, a voice from the shadows said, 'One moment please.'

Javert looked up and saw Monsieur Madeleine, one of the most important people in the town.

M. Madeleine had arrived mysteriously in Montreuil one December evening in 1815. He had no money but he had a revolutionary idea: he knew a cheap and efficient method of manufacturing glass. Within a few months of his arrival, thanks to his new idea, the glass-making factory in Montreuil was making enormous profits. With the money he made, M. Madeleine built two new factories, which provided the town with hundreds of new jobs. He became a very wealthy man but lived a simple life, using most of his money to build new hospitals and schools. He was so popular that, in 1820, the townspeople elected him mayor of Montreuil.

There was one man, however, who did not like M. Madeleine. This was the chief of police, Inspector Javert.

He had always been suspicious of M. Madeleine, and was sure that he had seen him somewhere before, many years earlier. But he kept his suspicions to himself, not daring to say what he really believed: that M. Madeleine was, in fact, a dangerous criminal with a terrible past.

Now, years later, M. Madeleine was in the police station, trying to save Fantine from prison. Fantine, however, was not grateful. In fact, when she saw who it was, she spat at him.

'You own the factory where I used to work!' she shouted at him. 'I lost my job because of you. Now I've become a bad woman, but what choice did I have? I'll never get my daughter back if I don't make money.'

The mayor turned to Inspector Javert and said, in a soft, firm voice, 'This woman must be released.'

'That's impossible,' Javert replied. 'She attacked a man in the street, a respectable citizen. And now I've just seen her spit at you, the mayor of our town. A woman like this deserves to be punished.'

'But I saw what happened in the street just now,' M. Madeleine said. 'It was the man's fault, not this woman's. You should arrest him, not her.'

Javert argued with M. Madeleine for some time, but finally gave in. He walked angrily out of the room, leaving the mayor and the prostitute alone together. Fantine trembled, as confused as Javert had been. The man who had just saved her from prison was also the man who had caused all her troubles. The devil had suddenly decided to be kind, and she did not know what to think.

'I heard what you said,' M. Madeleine said to her. 'I honestly didn't know that you had lost your job, but I'll try to help you now. I'll pay your debts and arrange for your child to return to you. I'll give you all the money you need. I'll make you happy again. And I promise that, in the eyes of God, you have never been a bad woman.'

Fantine gazed at M. Madeleine with tears in her eyes. After all her pain and suffering she had, for the first time in her life, found kindness in another human being. At last she would be cared for, and she could look forward to a life of happiness with Cosette. Without a word, she fell to her knees and kissed the back of M. Madeleine's hand.

M. Madeleine sent the Thénardiers 300 francs and told them to send Cosette to Montreuil immediately. Thénardier, thinking that Fantine had suddenly become rich, wrote back and demanded 500 francs. M. Madeleine sent the money, but the Thénardiers found even more dishonest excuses for not sending Cosette back.

◆

The weeks passed and, although she was happier than she had been for a long time, Fantine caught a fever. Months of poverty and misery had made her ill, and she soon became so weak that she was unable to leave her bed.

'When shall I see Cosette?' she kept asking M. Madeleine when he visited her.

'Very soon,' he would reply, and her pale face would light up with joy.

One morning, as M. Madeleine was making preparations to leave for Montfermeil and to fetch Cosette himself, he had a visitor. Inspector Javert walked into his office, and stood in silence waiting for him to look up from his work.

'Well, Javert, what is it?' M. Madeleine finally said.

'I've come to apologize, M. Madeleine,' the inspector replied.

'What are you talking about?'

'I've treated you unjustly. I was angry with you six weeks ago when you told me to release that woman. I wrote to the police headquarters in Paris and told them about you.'

'Told them *what* about me?'

'Forgive me, M. Madeleine, but I believed you were a man called Jean Valjean. He was a prisoner I saw twenty years ago, when I worked at a prison in Toulon. After being released from prison, this Valjean stole some silver from the Bishop of Digne and robbed a small boy on a public footpath. We tried to catch him, but he disappeared. When you arrived in Montreuil, I felt sure that you were this man, but now I know I was wrong, and I'm sorry. You will, of course, dismiss me from my job, as I've shown that I don't deserve your trust.'

M. Madeleine, looking hard at Javert without expression, said quietly, 'I'm afraid I don't understand.'

'The police headquarters in Paris told me that Jean Valjean was arrested last autumn for stealing apples,' Javert explained. 'He'd changed his name to Champmathieu and had lived for several years in the village of Ailly-le-Haut-Cloche. Two ex-prisoners from Toulon recognized him as Jean Valjean. I visited the man in Arras prison, and I saw for myself that he is indeed Jean Valjean. Of course, he denies everything, but that's not surprising. If he's found guilty of stealing from the bishop – who, as you know, died a couple of years ago – and of robbing the small boy, he'll spend the rest of his life in prison.'

M. Madeleine looked down at his papers.

'This matter is of no interest to me, Javert,' he said casually. 'I'm sure you have other work to do.'

'I was going to the man's trial in Arras tomorrow,' Javert said. 'But after this conversation, you must dismiss me.'

M. Madeleine rose to his feet.

'Javert,' he said, 'you're an honourable man. You made one small mistake, that's all. I want you to continue your excellent work as inspector of police.'

He offered Javert his hand, but the inspector refused to take it. Instead, he said, 'I've behaved unjustly towards an innocent man. I cannot shake his hand.'

With those words he bowed and left the office, leaving M. Madeleine to stare at the papers on his desk with an empty, puzzled look in his eyes.

That afternoon, M. Madeleine visited Fantine. She had a high fever, and was coughing badly, but she still had only one thing on her mind.

'Cosette?' she asked him.

'Very soon,' he assured her.

He sat by her bed for an hour and then, having told the nurses to look after her, he returned to his home. He stayed awake all night, thinking of Javert's story about Champmathieu. The reader has probably already realized that M. Madeleine was really Jean Valjean, and M. Madeleine – as we shall continue to call him for this part of the story – knew that he could not let Champmathieu go to prison for crimes he had not committed. He knew – although he was not happy to admit this – that he would have to go to Arras and tell the truth. He would lose everything that he had worked so hard to achieve. He would also have to break his promise to Fantine about bringing Cosette from Montfermeil. But what choice did he have? The truth was more important than anything else.

◆

The next morning, M. Madeleine set off on the long journey to Arras. It took him more than twelve hours, and when he arrived, he discovered that Champmathieu's trial had already started. The courtroom was full but, because he was such an important man, M. Madeleine was allowed to sit behind the judge's chair. He watched as several witnesses swore on the Bible that the man standing before the judge was Jean Valjean. Champmathieu, a large, simple-minded man, denied everything when his chance came to speak, but the crowd thought he was trying to be funny. The courtroom filled with laughter and Champmathieu began to laugh himself, which did him no good at all.

Finally, having heard all the evidence, the judge called for silence. He was preparing to announce his decision when M. Madeleine, pale and trembling, stood up and said:

'That man is not Jean Valjean.'

An excited whisper went around the courtroom as everybody recognized M. Madeleine.

M. Madeleine waited for the whispers to stop before announcing in a loud, clear voice that *he* was Jean Valjean. At first, no one believed him, but he managed to persuade the court by skilfully questioning each of the witnesses, revealing personal information that only the real Jean Valjean could have known. When he had persuaded the court of the truth of his confession, he was faced with a shocked but respectful silence.

'I must leave now,' M. Madeleine finally said. 'I have important business to attend to. You know where to find me, and I shall not try to escape.'

Everybody stood to one side to let him pass as he made his

way towards the door. When he had gone, the judge immediately allowed Champmathieu to leave the court a free man. Champmathieu went home in a state of total confusion, thinking all men mad and understanding nothing of what had happened.

♦

At dawn the next day, M. Madeleine entered Fantine's room.

'How is she?' he asked the nurse, who was watching her as she slept.

'She seems better. She's looking forward to seeing her child.'

'I haven't brought the child with me,' M. Madeleine said.

'Then what can we say to her when she wakes up?' The nurse looked suddenly worried. 'It will destroy her if she doesn't see her child now, after you promised to bring her.'

'God will guide me,' M. Madeleine sighed.

For some time M. Madeleine sat by the bedside and watched Fantine while she slept. She was breathing with great difficulty, but her face looked peaceful and calm. Suddenly, she opened her eyes and saw M. Madeleine.

'Cosette?' she asked, with a soft smile.

'Later,' M. Madeleine said gently, taking her hand. 'You're too weak to see her at the moment. First you must get well.'

Fantine smiled, and began to talk dreamily about her future life with her daughter, and how happy they would be together. But suddenly her face froze, and she stared with horror at the door. M. Madeleine, who was holding her hand, turned and saw Inspector Javert. Fantine, thinking that the inspector had come for her, gripped M. Madeleine's hand tightly and begged him to protect her.

'Don't be afraid.' M. Madeleine tried to calm her. 'He hasn't come for you.' Then, gently rising from his chair, he moved towards Javert. 'I know what you've come for,' he said quietly so that Fantine wouldn't hear. 'But give me three days, please. That's all I ask. Three days to fetch this unfortunate woman's child. I'll pay anything you like.'

'Do you think I'm stupid?' Javert gave an unpleasant laugh. 'Three days to escape, you mean.'

Fantine, who had heard what M. Madeleine said, despite his efforts to speak quietly, began to tremble.

'To fetch my child?' she cried. 'Isn't she here? Nurse, answer me ... where's my little Cosette? I want to see her. M. Madeleine ...'

'Be quiet, you dirty prostitute,' Javert interrupted her angrily. 'There is no Monsieur Madeleine. This man's name is Jean Valjean, and he's a criminal no better than you are. And you can forget all that nonsense about your child ...'

Fantine suddenly sat up. She stared wildly at the two men, then turned to the nurse. She looked as if she was going to speak, but no words came from her lips. Instead, with a small sigh, she fell back against her pillow and lay completely still.

Jean Valjean (as we must now call him) shook Javert's hand from his collar and ran to the bed. He gazed into Fantine's eyes and knew immediately that she was dead.

'You've killed her!' he cried angrily, turning to Javert with a fierce look in his eyes.

'I didn't come here to argue,' Javert said, stepping back nervously, afraid that Valjean was going to attack him. 'If you don't come with me now, I'll have to call my men.'

Valjean looked around the room, thinking for a second of making his escape. But the idea did not last for long. He turned again to Fantine and looked for one last time at her sad, pale face and empty, blue eyes. Bending down, he closed her eyes and pressed his lips against her forehead. Then he rose and turned back to Javert.

'I'm ready now,' he said.

News of M. Madeleine's arrest spread quickly around the

town. Most people pretended not to be surprised. 'We always knew there was something strange about him,' they said. Two days after his arrest, Jean Valjean escaped from prison. The bars of his window had been broken during the night. Again, most people pretended not to be surprised. 'It takes more than a small town prison to hold a man as strong as that,' they all agreed.

Chapter 4   The Man in the Long Yellow Coat

Christmas 1823 was especially lively and colourful in the village of Montfermeil. Entertainers and traders from Paris set up their stalls in the streets, and business at the Thénardiers' inn was very good. While guests and visitors ate and drank noisily, Cosette – now eight years old – sat in her usual place under the kitchen table. Dressed in rags, she knitted woollen stockings for Éponine and Azelma.

One evening, Madame Thénardier ordered Cosette out into the cold to fetch water. The nearest water supply was half-way down the wooded hill on which Montfermeil stood, and Cosette hated fetching water, especially in the dark. Miserably, she picked up a large, empty bucket that was almost as big as she was, and was walking with it to the door when Madame Thénardier stopped her.

'Buy some bread on the way,' she said, giving the girl some money.

Cosette took the coin, put it carefully in her pocket and left. She was cold and hungry as she dragged the bucket behind her along the crowded street, but she could not resist stopping in front of one of the stalls. It was like a palace to her, with its bright lights, shining glass and pretty objects. But the object that most attracted Cosette's attention was a large, golden-haired doll in a beautiful long pink dress. All the children in Montfermeil had gazed with wonder at this doll, but nobody in the village had enough money to buy it.

Cosette gazed at the doll for several minutes but, remembering her job, she sighed and continued on her way. She had soon left the colourful lights and the happy laughter of the village behind her, and was running down the hill into the frightening darkness of the wood. Finding the stream, she bent forward and began to fill her bucket. She did not notice the coin that Mme Thénardier had given her for the bread fall out of her pocket into the water. When the bucket was full, she gripped the handle with her tiny, frozen hands and tried to pull it back up the hill. But the bucket was so heavy that, after a dozen steps, she had to stop for a rest. She managed a few more steps, and stopped again. Her progress became slower and slower. She was almost at the end of her strength, and she was still not out of the wood. Leaning against a tree, she cried aloud:

'Oh God help me! Please, dear God!'

Suddenly, an enormous hand reached down from the sky and took the bucket of water from her. Looking up, Cosette saw a huge, white-haired man standing next to her. He looked very strange with his tall black hat and long yellow coat.

'This is a very heavy bucket for such a small child,' he said gently, looking down at her from his great height.

For some reason, Cosette was not afraid. There was something about his eyes, filled with a strange sadness, that she liked and trusted. She let him carry the bucket up the hill and, as they walked back towards the village, she told him everything about her life with the Thénardiers. The old man listened with great interest, and asked her many questions.

As they were approaching the inn, Cosette turned to him and said, 'May I have the bucket now? If Mme Thénardier sees that someone has been helping me, she'll beat me.'

The old man gave her the bucket, and they entered the inn together.

'What took you so long?' Mme Thénardier said angrily when she saw the little girl.

'This gentleman wants a room for the night,' Cosette said, trembling with fear, expecting to be beaten.

Mme Thénardier glanced at the old man without interest. She could tell from his clothes that he probably had no money.

'I'm sorry, the rooms are full,' she said.

'I can pay the price of a room,' the old man said.

'Forty sous,'* Mme Thénardier replied (although the usual price was twenty).

'Forty sous,' the man agreed.

He sat down and Cosette, after serving him some wine, returned to her place under the table. But before she could start her knitting, she heard Mme Thénardier's angry voice demanding, 'Where's the bread I told you to get?'

Cosette, who had forgotten about the bread, came out from under the table.

'The baker's was shut,' she lied.

'Well, give me back the money.'

Cosette felt in her pocket and suddenly went pale. The coin was not there.

'I'm waiting,' Mme Thénardier said threateningly.

Cosette said nothing, speechless with fear as the woman raised her arm to hit her. But before she could deliver the blow the old man, who had seen everything, interrupted her.

'Madame, I've just noticed this on the floor. It must have fallen from the child's pocket.'

Mme Thénardier took the coin the old man held towards her and walked away.

* sou: a small former French coin of little value.

At that moment the door opened and Éponine and Azelma appeared. They were two healthy girls, the old man noticed, dressed in warm clothes and with pink, healthy cheeks. After hugging and kissing their mother, they sat on the floor by the fire and played with a doll. Cosette, who had returned to her place under the table, looked up from her knitting and watched them sadly. A short time later, the girls grew bored with their game. They left the doll on the floor and went off to play with a baby cat. Cosette, checking that no one was watching, reached out and picked up the doll. She turned her back on the room and began to play with it, hoping that no one could see what she was doing. Her happiness did not last long, however. The two girls, when they saw Cosette with their doll, ran crying to their mother. Mme Thénardier rushed across the room towards Cosette who, afraid that she would be punished, put the doll gently on the floor and began to cry.

'What's the matter?' the old man said, rising to his feet.

'Can't you see?' Mme Thénardier said, red with anger. 'That nasty little girl, who isn't even my own daughter, who I feed and look after out of the kindness of my heart, has been playing with my daughters' doll.'

'I don't understand,' the old man said.

'She's touched it with her dirty hands!' Then, hearing Cosette crying, she turned to the little girl and shouted, 'Stop that noise!'

The old man left the inn and, minutes later, returned with something in his hands: the beautiful doll from the stall across the road.

'Here,' he said softly, placing it gently on the floor in front of Cosette. 'It's for you.'

There was a sudden silence in the room. Mme Thénardier, Éponine and Azelma stood absolutely still. The drinkers at the other tables paused, glasses half-way to their lips, and stared with disbelief.

'What kind of man is this?' they thought. 'He dresses so poorly but can afford to buy the most expensive doll in Montfermeil!'

The Thénardiers gave the old man their best room for the night. The next morning they gave him the bill, charging him three times the usual price for a meal and a bed for the night. They waited nervously while the man studied the bill carefully, expecting him to complain or cause trouble. Finally, he looked up from the bill without expression and said, 'Tell me, is business good here in Montfermeil?'

'Times are very hard,' Mme Thénardier replied immediately. 'This is a poor country. I don't know how we would manage without the occasional rich and generous traveller like yourself. We have so many expenses. That child, for instance – you've no idea how much she costs. We have our own daughters to look after. I can't afford to look after other people's children, too.'

'What would you say,' the old man said after a moment's thought, 'if I offered to take the child from you?'

'Oh!' Madame Thénardier's face brightened. 'That would be wonderful.'

'Just a minute,' her husband said. 'We love that child very much. It's true we're poor, and we have bad debts, but love is more important than money.'

'How much do you need?' the old man asked, taking an old leather wallet from the pocket of his coat.

'1500 francs,' Thénardier, who had already done his arithmetic, replied.

The old man put three 500-franc notes on the table and said, without smiling, 'Now fetch Cosette.'

When Cosette came downstairs, the old man gave her new clothes to wear: a black woollen dress, black stockings, scarf and shoes. Half an hour later, the people of Montfermeil saw an old man in a tall hat and long yellow coat walking along the road to Paris, hand-in-hand with a little girl dressed completely in black. No one knew the man. And, because she was carrying an expensive doll and was no longer wearing rags, not many recognized Cosette.

Cosette was leaving at last. She did not know where to, or with whom. But, as she held the old man's hand, she gazed wide-eyed at the sky. She had the strange but comforting feeling that she was somehow travelling closer to God.

Chapter 5   Valjean and Cosette

Somewhere on the outskirts of Paris, Jean Valjean stopped outside a large, ancient building with damp walls. He took a key from the pocket of his long yellow coat and opened the old wooden door. He then carried Cosette, who was sleeping in his arms, along a dark corridor and up some stairs to the room he had rented since his escape from Montreuil. There was not much furniture in the room – just an old bed, a mattress on the floor, a table, some chairs and a lighted stove. A streetlamp shone through the only window, lighting the dark interior of the room.

Valjean laid Cosette on the bed without waking her. He lit a candle and sat by the bed, watching her while she slept. He felt sad that Fantine had not lived to see her child again, but happy that he had been able to rescue her child from the terrible Thénardiers. He bent and kissed the sleeping child's forehead just as, nine months earlier, he had kissed her mother's.

The next morning, Cosette opened her eyes and immediately started to get out of bed.

'I'm coming, Madame,' she yawned, blinded by the bright winter's sunlight that was shining into the room.

Then, as her eyes adjusted to the light, she saw the kind old face of Jean Valjean looking down at her, and she relaxed.

'Of course!' she cried with joy. 'It's all true. I was afraid that it was just a dream.'

She hugged her doll and asked Valjean hundreds of questions. Finally, she asked him, 'Do you want me to sweep the floor?'

'No,' he said. 'I just want you to enjoy yourself.'

The December days passed in great happiness for Cosette and for Jean Valjean, too. For twenty-five years he had been alone in the world. Nothing had ever touched his heart until he had rescued Cosette. Now, he discovered the greatest joy he had ever known by just standing beside her bed and looking at her innocent, trusting little face. He had discovered love.

◆

After escaping from Montreuil, Jean Valjean had taken all his money from the bank and buried it in a forest near Montfermeil. Although he was rich, he had chosen a room in a poor part of Paris, where nobody would find him. His only neighbour was an old woman, who did his housework and kept his stove burning. Paying her six months in advance, he told her that he was a ruined Spanish gentleman, and that the little girl was his granddaughter.

Weeks passed, and the two lived happily. Valjean gave Cosette lessons in reading and writing, and spent hours watching her as she dressed and undressed her doll. To avoid being seen, he never went out during the day. He walked for a couple of hours every evening, sometimes alone, sometimes with Cosette. He often gave money to beggars, which was unwise, because he soon became known in the area as 'the beggar who gives money to beggars'.

One evening, towards the end of winter, Valjean gave some money to a beggar sitting under a streetlamp outside a church. The beggar raised his face and stared hard at Valjean for just a second, then quickly bowed his head. This gave Valjean a shock. Although he had only seen the beggar's face for a second, it had seemed strangely familiar.

'I'm going mad,' he thought, as he walked home.

The next evening he returned to the steetlamp outside the church. The beggar was still there, in the same position, wearing the same clothes. This time, Valjean spoke to him as he gave him some money. The beggar laughed and joked with him, and Valjean returned that evening a happier man.

'I must have been dreaming yesterday,' he laughed to himself. 'But for a second, there was something about the beggar's eyes that reminded me of Javert. How could I have thought such a thing? After speaking to him this evening, I can see that he doesn't look like the inspector at all.'

A few evenings later, while he was giving Cosette a reading lesson in his room, Valjean heard the front door of the house open and close. This was unusual. The old woman, the only other person who lived in the building, always went to bed before nightfall. Valjean signalled to Cosette to keep quiet. Someone was coming up the stairs. He blew out the candle and, just as he was kissing Cosette on the forehead, the footsteps stopped. Valjean did not move. He sat in his chair with his back to the door and held his breath. A few minutes later, having heard only silence, he turned round. A light was shining through a crack in his door. Someone with a candle was standing outside his room.

Several minutes passed, and then the light disappeared. Valjean quietly lay down on the mattress on his floor, but he could not close his eyes all night. At daybreak, as he was falling asleep at last, he heard footsteps in the corridor outside his room again. Running to the door, he put his eye to the large keyhole and saw the back view of a man who was walking towards the stairs. A tall man in a long coat with a stick under his arm.

Valjean's heart almost stopped beating and he began to sweat.

'Javert,' he breathed to himself.

◆

Valjean spent all day making preparations to leave. It was too dangerous for him and Cosette to stay there another night. That evening, he went downstairs and looked up and down the street. It seemed empty, although he could not see into the shadows behind the trees. He went back upstairs for Cosette, who was waiting for him patiently, holding her doll.

'Come along,' he said. 'It's time to leave.'

Cosette took his hand, and went with him down the stairs.

There was a full moon, and this pleased Valjean as he moved quickly along the narrow streets. By keeping close to the walls in the shadows, he could clearly see what was happening in the light. After a while, he felt confident that he and Cosette were not being followed. But, as the church bells of the city struck eleven o'clock, something made him look back. In the light of a lamp above a doorway, he saw four men moving along the street in his direction. He gripped Cosette's hand and began to walk more quickly. Every few minutes, he stopped in the shadows of a doorway or at the corner of a street to look back. The four men were still following him. He could see their faces clearly in the moonlight, and one of them belonged to Inspector Javert.

By now, Cosette was exhausted. Valjean picked her up and ran with her through a confusing system of alleys until he came to a bridge. On the other side of the river, he stopped at the entrance of a high-walled alley and looked back. He could see four figures in the distance on the far side of the bridge.

Walking more slowly now, thinking he was safe from his pursuers, Valjean followed the alley until he came to a lane that seemed to lead away from the city. He walked along this lane for a long time until, to his horror, he discovered his way blocked by a high wall. There was no way forward, but as he was turning back, he saw movements in the distance and the flash of moonlight on metal. Seven or eight soldiers were moving slowly along the lane in his direction.

Valjean looked desperately for an escape from the alley, but could see none. On one side of him was a tall building, all its doors and windows covered with metal bars. On the other side there was a wall, higher than a tree. He would be able to climb the wall on his own, but how could he carry Cosette? Suddenly, he had an idea. He ran to a nearby streetlight and pulled some wire from a metal box at its base. He tied one end of the wire around Cosette's waist, climbed the wall and, with great difficulty, pulled the girl up behind him. He was only just in time. There was a tree on the other side of the wall, and Valjean carried Cosette down into its branches just as the soldiers arrived.

'He must be here!' He heard Javert's voice clearly on the other side of the wall. 'He can't have escaped. There's no way out!'

At last, the soldiers gave up their search and went back in the direction they had come. Valjean hugged Cosette tightly with relief, knowing that at last they were both safe.

Chapter 6   Marius

On the night after the Battle of Waterloo, in June 1815, a robber moved quietly around the battlefield, stealing money and jewellery from the bodies of dead soldiers. He saw a hand sticking out from a pile of dead men and horses, a gold ring on its middle finger, shining in the moonlight. The robber took the ring but, as he turned to leave, the hand grabbed his jacket. The robber pulled the body from the pile of bodies and saw that he had rescued a French officer. The man had a terrible wound in his head, but he was still alive.

'Thank you,' the officer whispered. 'You've saved my life. What's your name?'

'Thénardier,' the robber replied.

31

'I shall not forget that name,' the officer replied. 'And you must remember mine. My name's Pontmercy.'

Without another word, the robber took the wounded man's watch and purse, and disappeared into the night.

Georges Pontmercy was married with a young son. He survived the Battle of Waterloo but unfortunately, in the same year, his wife died. His father-in-law, M. Gillenormand, was a very wealthy man, but the two men hated each other. M. Gillenormand hated everybody who liked Napoleon. He thought that Pontmercy was no better than a beggar, a penniless adventurer who only wanted his money. Pontmercy thought that M. Gillenormand was an old fool. When his daughter died, M. Gillenormand made Pontmercy an offer which he could not refuse.

'You have no money, and I am rich,' he said. 'If you want to keep your son, Marius, I'll give you no money. But if you give the boy to me, and promise never to see him again, I'll look after him.'

Pontmercy, wanting his son to have a good life, had sadly given him to M. Gillenormand and never saw his son or father-in-law again.

Marius grew up with his grandfather, and never knew his father. M. Gillenormand always told him that his father had been no good – that he was a poor soldier and a drunk who had abandoned him after his mother's death. For many years, Marius believed this, but when he was seventeen years old, he learnt the truth. His father, a brave officer who had fought for Napoleon and nearly died at the Battle of Waterloo, had really loved him and his mother very much. Without telling his grandfather, Marius tried to contact his father and finally discovered where he was living. He went at once to visit him, but he was too late. His father had just died. A poor man, Georges Pontmercy had left his son nothing apart from a letter:

For my son. My life was saved at Waterloo by a sergeant. His name was Thénardier. I believe that he recently managed a small inn in the village of Montfermeil, not far from Paris. If you ever find this man, I want you to help him in any way you can.

Marius returned to Paris, but continued to visit his father's grave regularly, without telling his grandfather. One day, however, his grandfather discovered what he was doing. They had a big quarrel, and M. Gillenormand ordered Marius to leave his house.

◆

For the next three years, Marius lived in a small room in an old, damp-walled building on the outskirts of Paris – the same room that Valjean and Cosette had lived in eight years earlier. He gave up studying law and earned his living by working in a bookshop and helping to write dictionaries. He did not earn very much money, but it was enough for the rent and simple meals. He rarely bought new clothes, but he was proud of the fact that he had never been in debt. His grandfather often tried to send him money, but Marius always returned it. He hated his grandfather for the unjust, cruel way he had treated his poor father. Life was hard for him, but he never forgot the promise he had made his father: that he would find Thénardier, the man who had saved his father's life, and help him in any way he could.

Marius was a handsome young man, but he was also extremely shy. When girls looked at him and smiled, he thought they were laughing at his old clothes. In fact, they were attracted by his good looks, but he was not confident enough to realize this. As a result, he had no girlfriend, but he was happy with his books.

'You shouldn't stay alone all the time,' his good friend, Enjolras, said to him. 'You should get out more. Give the girls a chance. They'd be good for you, Marius. Otherwise you'll turn into a priest!'

Marius paid little attention to his friend, and continued his quiet life of work, study and daily walks.

While walking around his part of the city, Marius had noticed an elderly man and a young girl in the Luxembourg Gardens. They always sat next to each other on the same bench. The man, who was perhaps sixty, had white hair and a serious but friendly-looking face. The girl, who was aged thirteen or fourteen, always wore the same badly-cut black dress. She was very thin, almost ugly, but Marius noticed that she had lovely blue eyes. They seemed to be father and daughter.

Marius saw this couple frequently on his regular walks in the Gardens. But, although he was very interested in them, they seemed not to notice him at all. The girl was always talking happily, while the man said very little. He just looked at the girl from time to time with an affectionate, fatherly smile.

Enjolras had often seen the couple, too.

'Do you know who they are?' Marius asked him one day.

'I call the man M. Leblanc, because of his white hair, and the girl Mlle Lanoire, because of her black dress,'* his friend replied.

◆

For almost a year, Marius saw the old man and the young girl daily in the same place at the same time. Then, for some reason, Marius stopped going to the Luxembourg Gardens. When he returned, one summer morning six months later, he saw the same couple sitting on the same bench, but something amazing had happened. The man was the same, but the thin, plain girl of six months earlier had become a beautiful young woman. Her rough black dress had been replaced by one of fine black silk. She had soft brown hair, pale, smooth skin, deep blue eyes and a lovely smile that lit up her face like sunshine.

She looked up when Marius passed for the second time, and gave him a casual glance. Marius, however, walked on, thinking of other things. For the next few days he passed the bench in the

* blanc and noir: the French words for white and black.

Gardens without looking at her. Then one day, as he was passing, thinking about nothing in particular, the girl looked up at him and their eyes met. A second later she looked away and Marius walked on but, in a strange way, he knew his life had changed. What he had experienced in that moment was not the honest, innocent gaze of a child. It was something more than that. Whatever it was, Marius sensed that, after that moment, his life would never be the same.

The next day, Marius returned to the Luxembourg Gardens wearing his best clothes. He walked around slowly, stopping to look at the ducks on the lake, then casually approached the bench where Mlle Lanoire and her father were sitting. As he walked past, he kept his eyes fixed on the girl, but she did not seem to notice him. She was talking quietly to her father, and Marius could hear the soft, exciting murmur of her voice. Without intending to, he stopped, turned round and walked past the bench again. He felt his face go red and his heart beat loudly in his chest. He was sure, this time, that she had watched him as he passed. He did not go back a third time, but sat down on a bench at the opposite end of the Gardens. He looked at the girl out of the corner of his eye. She seemed to fill the far end of the Gardens with a kind of blue mist. Taking a deep breath, he rose and was going to pass the bench for a third time when he stopped. He suddenly realized that, in his feverish state, he had forgotten about the old man. What would *he* be thinking when he saw a strange young man walking backwards and forwards in front of his bench? Without another thought, Marius left the Gardens and went home.

He returned the next morning and sat on a bench all day, pretending to read a book, not daring to go near the bench where the girl and her father were sitting. He did the same every day for two weeks. Towards the end of the second week, while Marius was sitting in his usual place, he looked up from his book

35

and his face went pale. Something had happened at the far end of the Gardens. M. Leblanc and his daughter had risen from their bench and were slowly walking in his direction. Marius shut his book, opened it again and made an effort to read. When he felt that they were near him, he looked up and saw that the girl was looking steadily at him with a soft, thoughtful gaze that made him tremble from head to foot.

He gazed after her until she had disappeared from sight, then rose to his feet and walked around, laughing and talking to himself. Finally he left the Gardens in the mad hope of seeing her in the street, but instead he met Enjolras, who invited him to a meal.

Every day for the next month, Marius went to the Luxembourg Gardens, excited by knowing that the girl was secretly looking at him, but too shy and embarrassed to know what to do. He avoided walking directly in front of the bench, partly from shyness, partly because he did not want to attract her father's attention. Sometimes he stood for half an hour in a place where her father could not see him, looking at her and enjoying the small, secret smiles she sent him.

But it seemed that M. Leblanc had begun to suspect what was happening because often, when Marius appeared, he got to his feet and walked away, taking his daughter with him. Sometimes M. Leblanc took his daughter to a different bench, to see if Marius would follow them. Marius failed to understand the trick, and made the mistake of doing so. Then M. Leblanc became irregular in his visits and did not always bring his daughter with him. When this happened, Marius did not stay in the Gardens, which was another mistake.

Marius was too much in love to think clearly. His desire for the girl was growing daily, and he dreamt of her every night. One evening, he found a handkerchief lying on the bench which M. Leblanc and his daughter had just left. It was a plain, white handkerchief with the initials *U.F.* in one corner.

'Ursula.' Marius said the first name that came into his head. 'A delicious name!'

He kissed the handkerchief, breathed in its perfume, wore it next to his heart by day and kept it under his pillow at night.

'I can feel her whole soul in it!' he told himself.

In fact, the handkerchief belonged to M. Leblanc and had simply fallen out of his pocket, but Marius was unaware of this. He never appeared in the Luxembourg Gardens without the handkerchief pressed to his lips or his heart. The girl could not understand his behaviour at all, and looked at him with a puzzled expression.

'Such modesty!' Marius sighed.

Eventually, Marius was not satisfied with just knowing the girl's name; he wanted to know where she lived. He found that she lived in a small house at the quiet end of the rue* de l'Ouest. As well as the joy of seeing her in the Gardens, he now had the pleasure of following her home. One evening, having followed them to the house and watched them enter, he went in after them and spoke to the concierge. The concierge, however, became suspicious, thinking that Marius was connected with the police, and refused to say anything.

The following day, M. Leblanc and his daughter did not come to the Gardens at all. They did not come for a whole week, and Marius began to feel depressed. Every night he stood outside their house and gazed up at their lighted windows. Sometimes he saw a shadow pass in front of a lamp, and his heart beat faster.

On the eighth night there was no light in the windows. Marius waited, his heart aching with pain, until finally going home. The next day they did not go to the Gardens, so again Marius went to the house as night was falling. Once again, there were no lights in the windows. He knocked on the door and spoke to the concierge.

* rue: the French word for street.

'Where's the old gentleman?' he asked.

'He's left.'

Marius felt the blood leave his face. Almost fainting, he asked in a weak voice, 'When did he leave?'

'Yesterday.'

'Where has he gone?'

'I've no idea.'

'Did he leave an address?'

The concierge then recognized Marius from the previous week. He stared fiercely at him and said, 'So, it's you again! I was right. You *are* some kind of policeman.'

With those words he slammed the door in Marius's face.

Chapter 7   The Jondrettes

Summer and autumn passed, and winter came, but Marius saw no sign of M. Leblanc or 'Ursula'. He searched everywhere for them, but without success. He became like a homeless dog, wandering the streets in a mood of dark despair. Without 'Ursula', his life had become meaningless, work disgusted him, walking tired him, solitude bored him.

'If only I hadn't followed them home,' he told himself. 'It gave me so much happiness just to look at her, and now, through my stupidity, I've lost even that.'

Enjolras and his other friends tried to cheer him up by taking him to exciting places, but these expeditions always ended in the same way: Marius would leave the group and walk around the streets of Paris unhappily on his own.

One cold but sunny afternoon in February, Marius was walking along the street when two young girls dressed in rags ran into him. One was tall and thin, the other smaller. From what they were shouting at each other, he understood that they were running from the police. He stood for a moment staring after them as they disappeared round a corner. Then he noticed a small parcel of papers lying on the ground.

Realizing that one of the girls must have dropped it, he picked it up and called after them, but it was too late. The girls had already disappeared from sight. With a sigh, he put the package in his pocket and went on to dinner.

That night at home, Marius opened the package and found that it contained four letters, all addressed to different people, and smelling strongly of cheap tobacco. Marius read the four letters and discovered that they were all asking for money. However, there was something strange about them: although they all seemed to be written by different people, they were written on the same rough paper in the same handwriting. He also noticed that each of them had similar spelling mistakes. Thinking no more about it, he wrapped the letters up again, threw them into a corner and went to bed.

The next morning, while he was working, there was a gentle knock on his door.

'Come in,' Marius said, expecting it to be the concierge, Mme Bougon. But the voice that answered, saying, 'I beg your pardon, Monsieur,' was not that of Mme Bougon. It was more like the voice of a sick old man.

Marius looked up quickly and saw that his visitor was a thin girl wearing just a skirt and shirt. She looked cold and ill, and when she spoke, Marius saw that she had lost several of her teeth. There was, however, still a trace of beauty in the sixteen-year-old face, like pale sunlight beneath the thick clouds of a winter's dawn. Marius rose to his feet, sure that he had seen the girl somewhere before.

'What can I do for you, Mademoiselle?' he asked.

'I've got a letter for you, M. Marius.'

Marius opened the letter and read:

My warm-hearted neighbour, I have heard of how you kindly paid my rent for me six months ago. I thank you for it. But my eldest daughter will tell you that my wife is sick and none of us have had any food for four days. Please, Monsieur, show us the kindness of your generous heart again. My daughter is at your service. Yours truly, Jondrette.

Marius realized at once that the handwriting, the yellow paper and the smell of cheap tobacco was the same as in the four letters he had read the previous evening. He now had five letters, all the work of one author: the man who lived with his family in the next room.

The Jondrette family had been Marius's neighbours for many months, but he had never before paid much attention to them. This was why he had failed to recognize the two daughters when they had run into him on the street. But now he understood that Jondrette's business was writing dishonest letters, asking for money from people he imagined were wealthier than himself.

Marius looked up from the letter and watched the girl moving fearlessly around his room, studying the furniture and the mirror on the wall. Her eyes lit up when she noticed the books on his writing desk.

'Books!' she said, and then added with pride, 'I know how to read and write. Look, I'll show you.'

Picking up a pen that lay on the table, she wrote on a piece of paper, *Be careful! The police are coming!* She showed Marius her work and then, changing the subject quickly, for no reason at all, she gazed into his eyes and said shyly, 'Do you know, M. Marius, that you're a very handsome boy?'

Approaching him, she rested a cold red hand on his shoulder and said, 'You never notice me, M. Marius, but I know you. I see you on the stairs, and I see you walking around the streets, looking so sad and alone.'

Marius's cheeks went red. He moved away from the girl's

touch and said, 'I think, Mademoiselle, that I have something belonging to you.' He handed her the parcel of letters.

She clapped her hands and cried, 'We've been looking for that everywhere! How did you know they were mine? Of course, the handwriting. You were the man we ran into last night.'

While she talked excitedly, she took out one of the letters. 'Ah, this is for the old man who goes to church every day. If I hurry, I might be able to catch him. Perhaps he'll give me enough for a dinner. We haven't eaten for three days . . .'

Marius took a five-franc piece from his pocket and handed it to the girl.

'The sun's come out at last!' she cried, eagerly accepting the coin. 'That's enough food for two days. You're a real gentleman, Monsieur.'

With those words, she gave a little laugh and wave, grabbed some dry bread from the table and disappeared out of the door.

♦

Marius had lived for five years without much money, but he had never been really poor. Now, after his conversation with the girl from the next room, he understood what real poverty was. Only a thin wall separated him from the family of lost souls in the room next door. He had heard them and seen them, but had paid them no attention, and he suddenly felt guilty.

'If they had had another neighbour,' he thought, 'one who had noticed their suffering, perhaps they could have been rescued by now.'

As Marius was thinking about the sad life of the family in the next room, he stared dreamily at the wall that separated them. Then, in the top corner near the ceiling, Marius saw that there was a triangular hole.

'Let's see what these people are really like,' Marius thought. 'Then I'll be in a better position to help them.'

He stood on a cupboard, put his eye to the hole, and looked through it into his neighbours' room.

The Jondrettes' room was dirty and evil-smelling, unlike Marius's bare but clean room. Its only furniture was a chair, an old table, some cracked dishes and two dirty beds, one on each side of a fireplace. A man with a long, grey beard was sitting at the table, writing a letter and smoking a pipe. A large woman with greying hair, once red, was sitting by the fire, while a thin, pale-faced child sat on one of the beds.

Marius, depressed at what he saw, was going to get down from the cupboard when the door of the Jondrettes' room opened and the elder girl came in. Slamming the door shut behind her she cried victoriously, 'He's coming!'

'Who's coming?' Her father looked up.

'The old man who goes to church. He's following me. I saw him with his daughter in the church, and gave him the letter. He said he would follow me here. I ran ahead to tell you he'll be here in two minutes.'

'You're a good girl,' the man said, rising quickly to his feet. Then, turning to his wife, he said, 'Quickly! Put out the fire!' While she poured water on the flames, the man broke the chair with his foot and told his younger daughter to break a window. She put her fist through the glass and ran to her bed, crying because her arm was covered in blood.

'Excellent,' her father smiled, tearing a piece off his shirt and using it as a bandage. 'Now we're ready for the kind gentleman. When he sees how miserable we are, he'll give us a lot of money, you'll see.'

Moments later, there was a gentle knock on the door. Jondrette rushed to open it, bowing almost to the ground as he did so.

'Please come in, my dear sir! Please enter, with your charming young lady.'

An elderly man and a young girl appeared in the doorway and Marius, still looking through the hole in the wall, could not believe his eyes.

It was She.

She! Everyone who has ever loved will feel the force of that small word. In the bright mist that clouded his vision, Marius could hardly see the features of the sweet face that had lit his life for six months and had then disappeared, filling his life with darkness. And now the vision had reappeared!

When Marius had recovered some of his senses, he saw that she seemed a little paler than before. Her companion as usual was M. Leblanc. As she entered the room, she put a large parcel on the table.

'Monsieur, you will find some woollen stockings and blankets in the parcel,' M. Leblanc told Jondrette.

'You are extremely generous, Monsieur,' Jondrette said, again bowing to the ground. 'But as you can see, we are unfortunate in many ways. We are without food, Monsieur, and without heating. No warmth for my unhappy children. Our only chair is broken. A broken window – in this weather! My wife ill in bed and our younger daughter injured.'

'Oh, the poor child,' 'Ursula' said, seeing the girl's bleeding wrist.

'She had an accident in the machine-shop where she works for six sous an hour,' Jondrette explained. 'They may have to cut off her arm.'

The daughter, taking her father's words seriously, began to scream with fear. While M. Leblanc and 'Ursula' tried to comfort her, Jondrette approached his wife and said in a whisper, 'Take a good look at that man.'

He then returned to M. Leblanc and told him about his debts.

'I owe sixty francs in rent,' he said.

M. Leblanc took a coin out of his pocket and put it on the table.

'Five francs is all I have with me,' he said. 'But I'll take my daughter home and come back this evening with more money for you.'

Jondrette accompanied M. Leblanc and 'Ursula' out of the door and, after a few minutes' indecision, Marius jumped down from the cupboard and ran out into the street. But he was too late; their carriage had already gone. Miserably, he turned back to the house. He went into his room, pushing the door behind him, but the door would not shut. Turning, Marius saw that a hand was holding it open.

'What is it?' he demanded.

It was the Jondrette girl.

'So it's you again,' he said almost fiercely. 'What do you want now?'

She did not reply but stood thoughtfully looking at him, seeming to have lost all her earlier confidence. She had not entered the room, but was still standing in the half-light of the corridor.

'What do you want?' Marius repeated angrily.

'M. Marius,' she said at last, a faint light in her sad eyes, 'you seem upset. What's the matter?'

'Nothing. Now please leave me alone.' Marius tried again to shut the door, but she still held it open.

'You're making a mistake,' she said. 'You aren't rich, but you were generous this morning. You've been kind to us – now I want to be kind to you. Is there anything that I can do?'

Marius considered her offer, then had an idea. Moving closer to her, he said, 'Do you know the address of those people who've just left your room?'

'No.'

'Can you find out for me?'

'Is that what you want?' she said, a disappointed look on her face.

'Yes.'

The girl looked hard at him for a minute.

'What will you give me?' she said at last.

'Anything you want.'

'Anything?'

'Yes.'

'Then I'll get it.'

She left immediately, closing the door behind her.

Marius sat down and buried his face in his hands, too overcome by emotion to think clearly. But then he heard a loud voice from the next room.

'I tell you I'm sure.' Jondrette was speaking to his wife. 'I recognized him.'

Without another thought, Marius jumped on to the cupboard and looked again through the hole in the wall.

'Really?' His wife looked puzzled. 'Are you sure?'

'Of course I'm sure. It's been eight years, but I recognized him at once.'

He told the two girls to leave the room and then, when alone with his wife, he said, 'And I recognized the girl too. I'm surprised you didn't.'

'Why should I? I've never seen her . . .'

But Jondrette bent down and whispered something in her ear. Straightening up, he said, 'Now do you recognize her?'

'*Her*?' said the woman, her voice filled with sudden hatred. 'Are you sure? That's impossible!' she cried. 'Our daughters barefoot and without a dress between them, while *she* wears leather boots and a fur coat? You must be wrong. You've forgotten, that child was ugly, and this one's not bad-looking.'

'I tell you, it's the same girl. You'll see. And I'll tell you another thing. She's going to make us a fortune. I'm tired of being poor. We deserve a better life, and this is our chance.'

'What do you mean?'

'He said he'll be here at six o'clock, with sixty francs. I'll bring some friends round, and we'll make sure he gives us a lot more money.'

'What will you do if he doesn't give you more money?'

Jondrette stroked his beard and laughed. 'We'll know what to do about it.' And then, as he was going to leave the room, he turned to his wife and said, 'You know, it's lucky he didn't recognize me. If he had, he wouldn't be coming back here again. It's the beard that saved me – my lovely, long, romantic beard!'

With an ugly laugh, he pulled his cap down over his eyes and left the room.

◆

Although Marius was a dreamer and not a man of action, he knew immediately that he had to save M. Leblanc and 'Ursula' from the trap that Jondrette was setting for them. But what could he do? He could not warn M. Leblanc because he did not know the old man's address. There was only one thing to do: he had to tell the police.

Half an hour later, Marius was at the nearest police station.

The desk clerk showed him into the police chief's office, where a tall man with a wide face and a thin, tight mouth was trying to keep warm next to a fire.

'Are you the chief of police?' Marius asked.

'He's away,' the tall man said. 'I'm Inspector Javert. Now, what do you want?'

Marius told Javert about the morning's events. When he told Javert his address, he noticed the inspector's eyes light up with great interest. Then, when everything had been explained, Javert thought for a moment. Finally, he asked Marius for his door key and told him to go home and hide quietly in his room so that his neighbours would think he was out.

'Take these with you,' the inspector went on, producing two

small guns. 'When the old man and the girl arrive, let them start their business. When you think it's getting dangerous, shoot one of these guns. After that, I'll take charge.'

Back in his room, Marius sat down nervously on his bed. It was nearly six o'clock. Outside it had stopped snowing, and a full moon was growing steadily brighter above the mist. Suddenly, he heard voices. Taking off his boots, he quietly climbed on to the cupboard and looked through the hole in the wall. A fire burned in the corner of the room, filling it with blood-red light. Jondrette, who had just come in, was shaking snow from his shoes.

'Everything's arranged,' he said. 'Has the concierge gone out?'

'Yes,' his wife said.

'And you're sure he's not in next door?'

'Positive.'

'Good.' Then he turned to his daughters. 'Now, you two must go and keep guard in the street, one by the gate, one at the street corner.'

'A fine job!' the elder girl called back. 'Keeping guard barefoot in the snow.'

'Tomorrow you'll have fur boots!' her father called out after her.

A few minutes later, there was nobody in the building except for Marius and the Jondrettes. Marius watched as Jondrette put a metal bar in the fire and inspected a rope ladder on the table. Next, he opened a drawer, took out a long knife and tested its blade with his finger. Suddenly, at exactly six o'clock, the door into the Jondrettes' room opened.

'Welcome, Monsieur,' Jondrette said, rising to his feet.

M. Leblanc appeared and put four coins on the table. 'That is for your rent and food, Monsieur,' he said. 'Now we must discuss what else is needed.'

Jondrette quietly told his wife to dismiss the carriage, and when she had left the room, turned back to his visitor.

'How is the wounded child?' M. Leblanc asked him.

'Not well.' Jondrette smiled sadly. 'She's in great pain. Her sister has taken her to hospital, but they'll be back soon.'

The conversation continued politely in this way for several minutes. M. Leblanc asked Jondrette about his circumstances, and Jondrette smiled sadly as he invented lie after lie. Finally, Jondrette picked up a large picture that was leaning against the wall, and showed it to M. Leblanc.

'What's that?' M. Leblanc said, looking at the badly-drawn picture of a soldier in uniform.

'It's a work of art,' Jondrette informed him. 'I love this picture as much as I love my two daughters. But, unfortunately, I have to sell it. What do you think it's worth?'

'It's just an old inn-sign. It's worth about three francs.'

'I'll accept a thousand,' Jondrette softly replied.

M. Leblanc rose and, standing with his back to the wall, looked quickly round the room. Jondrette was on his left, his wife was standing on his right near the door. Jondrette put the picture down and stepped quietly towards the old man.

'You don't recognize me, do you?' he said in a loud, clear voice.

At this signal, which he had pre-arranged with his friends, three men armed with metal poles rushed into the room. M. Leblanc grew pale, and gripped the back of the broken chair with his huge hands. Marius, meanwhile, raised his right hand with the gun, ready to fire the warning shot.

'The carriage is ready?' Jondrette asked the three men.

'Yes, with two good horses,' one of them replied.

'Excellent.' He turned to M. Leblanc and repeated his earlier question. 'You still don't recognize me, do you?'

'No.'

'My name isn't Jondrette. It's Thénardier. Now do you recognize me?'

M. Leblanc trembled slightly, but still shook his head. Marius, however, who had been going to fire the gun as a signal for the police to arrive, shook so much that he almost fell off the cupboard.

'Thénardier,' he thought. 'That's the name of the man who saved my father's life at the Battle of Waterloo. The man I've promised to help!'

If he fired the warning shot, M. Leblanc would be saved and Thénardier would be destroyed. But he would also have broken his promise to his father. He felt his knees grow weak. What should he do?

Thénardier walked up and down in front of M. Leblanc.

'Do you remember the little inn in Montfermeil eight years ago? You took away our Cosette, do you remember? Wearing that old yellow coat, pretending you were a tramp! Well, now you're going to learn that you can't make things right by just bringing a few hospital blankets! You're the cause of all my troubles. For 1500 francs you took away a girl who was bringing me lots of money.'

'I don't know what you're talking about,' M. Leblanc said. 'I don't know who you are, but I know *what* you are. You're a dirty criminal.'

'A criminal?' Thénardier said, suddenly angry. 'That's what you rich people call people like me, isn't it? Just because I've failed in business. I was a war hero, you know – I saved an officer's life at Waterloo! And you call me a criminal! Well, I'm going to teach you a lesson.'

He began to move towards M. Leblanc, but the old man was too quick for him. With surprising speed, he pushed the table and chair to one side and ran to the window. He managed to open it but, before he could jump, the three men jumped on him and held him to the floor.

This was too much for Marius.

'Forgive me, father,' he murmured, preparing to fire the gun. But suddenly Thénardier cried, 'Don't hurt him!'

After a long fight, M. Leblanc was tied up and taken to the bed. 'No wallet?' Thénardier cried, having searched his pockets. 'Never mind.' He sat on the bed next to the helpless but brave old man, and said, 'Let's discuss things quietly. All I'm asking for is 200,000 francs. I realize that you don't have the money with you now, but I want you to write a letter. I'll tell you what to say.'

He untied M. Leblanc's right hand and, producing a pen and paper, began:

My dearest daughter, You must come at once. I need you urgently. The person who gives you this note will bring you to me. I shall be waiting.

M. Leblanc signed his name Urbain Fabre, which seemed to satisfy Thénardier, and wrote an address on the envelope. Thénardier then took the letter and gave it to his wife.

'There's a carriage outside. Don't be long.'

Nearly half an hour passed. Thénardier seemed lost in his own dark thoughts. The prisoner did not move. Finally, there was the sound of horses in the street outside and, moments later, the door to the room was thrown open.

'It's a false address,' Mme Thénardier cried. 'There's no Urbain Fabre. The old man's been lying to us!'

Thénardier sat on the corner of the table in silence for some moments, swinging his leg and gazing with a fierce satisfaction at the fire. Then he turned to the prisoner and said in a slow, threatening voice, 'What did you hope to gain by giving me a false name and address?'

'Time!' cried the prisoner in a loud voice, jumping from the bed, having secretly cut the ropes that tied him. Before the others in the room could react, M. Leblanc was standing by the fire, holding a metal bar above his head.

'I'm not afraid of you,' he said. 'But neither should you fear me.'

With those words he threw the metal bar out of the window into the street below.

'Get him!' Thénardier shouted. 'He's defenceless.'

Two men grabbed him by the shoulders.

'Now cut his throat!' Thénardier called.

Marius stared, frozen with fear as Thénardier, knife in hand, stood hesitating a few steps away from the prisoner. The brave man was in terrible danger, but Marius still could not fire the gun. Then, in the moonlight, he saw the solution to his problem. On top of the cupboard, by his feet, he noticed the piece of paper that the elder daughter had written on: *Be careful! The police are coming!*

He immediately saw what he had to do. He took a piece of brick from the wall, wrapped the piece of paper around it and threw it through the hole into the middle of Thénardier's room.

He was just in time. Thénardier was advancing towards his prisoner, knife in hand, when his wife cried, 'Something fell!'

She picked up the piece of paper and handed it to her husband, who read it quickly.

'It's Éponine's handwriting!' he cried a moment later. 'Quick! Get the ladder. The police are coming and we've got to go!'

They threw the rope ladder from the open window but, before they could escape, the door opened and Inspector Javert walked in.

'Relax,' he smiled. 'You can't escape through the window. There are five of you, and fifteen of us. You have no chance. Why not come quietly?'

The men put down their weapons and surrendered without a fight. When everybody had been arrested and taken from the room, Javert noticed the prisoner, who was standing, head bowed, by the window. He turned to speak to another policeman but, when he looked back, he saw that the prisoner had gone. Javert rushed to the open window and looked down. The rope ladder was swinging gently above the empty street.

'He must have been the cleverest of them all,' Javert murmured angrily to himself.

Chapter 8   Marius and Cosette

Not wishing to give evidence against Thénardier in court, Marius made immediate arrangements to leave his room. Early the following morning, he paid the concierge his final rent and went to live with his friend, Enjolras. Inspector Javert looked for Marius everywhere, but without success.

Two months later, Marius was deeply unhappy. He sent money every Monday to Thénardier, who was in prison, which meant that he had even less money for himself. But the main reason for his unhappiness was that he was forced to live his life with no hope of seeing 'Ursula'.

One afternoon he was sitting in a field, looking down at a small river, when his dreams of 'Ursula' were suddenly broken by the sound of a familiar voice. He looked up and recognized Éponine, Thénardier's elder daughter. Still wearing the same rags, with the same bold look in her eyes and the same rough voice, she had somehow become more beautiful. She stared at Marius with a look of pleasure on her pale face, and for some moments seemed unable to speak.

'So at last I've found you,' she finally said. 'I've been looking for you everywhere. You aren't living in the same room any more?'

'No,' said Marius.

'Well, I can understand that. It's not nice, that sort of thing. But why are you wearing that dirty old hat?' When Marius gave no answer, she went on, 'And you've got a hole in your shirt. I'll mend it for you. A young man like you ought to be nicely dressed.'

Marius still said nothing, and after a moment's pause she said, 'You don't seem very glad to see me, but I could make you look happy if I wanted to!'

'How?' said Marius. 'What do you mean?'

'You weren't so unfriendly last time.'

'I'm sorry, but what do you mean?'

She bit her lip and hesitated, as if trying to make up her mind about something. Finally, she said, 'I've got the address.'

Marius's heart seemed to miss a beat. 'You mean . . .'

'The address you wanted me to find out. The young lady, you know . . .' Her voice sank into a sigh.

Marius jumped up and took her by the hand.

'Let's go at once!' he cried, wild with excitement. Then he suddenly frowned and seized Éponine by the arm. 'But you must promise me,' he said, 'that you'll never tell your father the address.'

'I promise,' the girl replied, staring at Marius with amusement.

They had only gone a few steps when Éponine stopped and said, 'You remember you promised me something?'

Marius felt in his pocket. All he had in the world was the five-franc piece he intended to give her father in prison. He pushed it into her hand, but she opened her fingers and let the coin fall to the ground. She looked at him with a mixture of disappointment and sadness in her eyes.

'I don't want your money,' she said.

◆

That evening, Cosette was alone in the house which Jean Valjean had bought about a year earlier. It was a small house in a back street, with a large, wild garden. Valjean had gone away on business for a couple of days, and Cosette was in the downstairs sitting room, playing the piano.

Suddenly, she thought she heard the sound of footsteps in the garden. She listened at the window for a minute, then ran up to her bedroom, opened the window and looked out. The moonlit garden and the street beyond it were completely empty. Cosette, not a nervous girl by nature, smiled to herself and thought no more about it.

The next evening, as she was walking in the garden, she was sure that she heard someone moving in the trees. Again, when she looked round, she saw nothing. When Jean Valjean returned from his business the following day, Cosette told him about the noises in the garden. He told her not to worry, but she noticed an anxious look in his eyes. He spent the next two nights walking around the garden, checking the gate, listening for noises, but nothing unusual happened.

Then one morning, a few days later, Cosette noticed a large stone lying on the garden bench. Nervously, she picked it up and discovered an envelope underneath it. Inside, there was a small notebook filled with love poems. Cosette sat down and began to read, enjoying the music of the language and the beauty of the handwriting. She had never read anything like this before, and it affected her deeply.

Her heart on fire, she took the notebook upstairs to her bedroom and read every word again. She remembered the handsome young man she had seen so often in the Luxembourg Gardens. As she read the notebook, she knew in her heart that he was the author of these beautiful, romantic words. Finally, she kissed the book, held it to her heart and waited for the evening, when she knew that something special was going to occur.

That evening, Jean Valjean went out. Cosette spent a long time in front of the mirror, making her hair look beautiful and deciding which dress to wear. Finally, she went out into the garden. She sat on the bench where she had found the notebook and, moments later, had the strange feeling that she was being watched. She looked round and jumped to her feet.

It was He!

He looked paler and thinner than she remembered. His dark clothes were almost invisible in the shadows, and his face shone softly in the fading light. Cosette felt suddenly faint, but she did not move or make a sound.

'Forgive me for being here.' Marius spoke at last. 'But I've been so unhappy. Do you recognize me? You mustn't be afraid. It's a long time ago, but do you remember the day when you first looked at me – in the Luxembourg Gardens? And the day you walked past me? Those things happened nearly a year ago. Forgive me for talking like this, I don't know what I'm saying – perhaps I'm annoying you? But the truth is, I can't live without you.'

'Mother!' Cosette murmured, and began to fall.

Marius caught her and held her tightly in his arms without realizing what he was doing, lost in a mist of love. Cosette, feeling her body close to his, took his hand and pressed it against her heart. Aware of the shape of the notebook under her dress, he said, 'So, you've read my notebook. Do you love me, too?'

'Of course,' she answered in a low voice. 'You know I do.'

Then, as if by magic, her lips were next to his and they were kissing. Afterwards, they sat together on the garden bench in a state of shock, neither of them speaking. Beneath the stars, they were happy just to look into each other's eyes and hold each other's hands. Then, at last, they began to speak. They talked all evening about their dreams, their mistakes, their moments of happiness, their moments of despair. When everything had been said, she laid her head on his shoulder and asked, 'What's your name?'

'My name's Marius. And yours?'

'Cosette.'

During that month of May in the year 1832, Cosette and Marius met every day in the wild garden of that small, secret house. They would sit and hold hands and talk, or just gaze into each other's eyes and smile.

'How lovely you are,' Marius would sigh. 'There are moments when I think this is a dream. There are other moments when I think I'm a little mad. I love you so much.'

To which Cosette would reply, 'I love you more with every minute that passes.'

In this way, bathed in happiness, they lived untroubled by the world.

◆

One beautiful, starry evening, Marius found Cosette sitting unhappily in her garden.

'What's the matter?' he asked, sitting next to her on the bench.

'My father said that we may have to leave,' she replied.

Marius trembled. For six weeks, he had known nothing but uncomplicated happiness. Now, for the first time, there was a cloud in the clear blue sky of his life. He could not speak, and Cosette felt his hand grow cold.

She asked, as he had done, 'What's the matter?'

He replied, in a voice so low that she could hardly hear it, 'I don't understand what you mean.'

'Father told me this morning that I have to pack everything and be ready to leave for England within a week.'

Marius rose to his feet and said coldly, 'Cosette, are you going?'

She looked up at him, her pale face lined with misery.

'What else can I do?' she cried.

'So you're leaving me.'

'Oh, Marius, why are you being so cruel to me?'

Marius turned his back to her and said, 'Then I shall have to go away.'

'No, Marius, wait. I've got an idea.'

Marius turned and was surprised to see her smiling.

'What is it?'

'If we go, you must come too. I'll tell you where, and you must meet me there, wherever it is.'

'How can I possibly do that?' he cried. 'Are you crazy? You need money to go to England, and I haven't got any. I haven't told you, Cosette, but I'm a poor man. I wear a cheap hat, my jacket has lost half its buttons and there are holes in my boots.' He turned away from her and stood with his face pressed to the trunk of a tree, almost ready to faint. He stayed in that position for some time. Finally, he heard a small sound behind him and, turning round, he saw that Cosette was in tears.

He fell on his knees in front of her and pressed her hand to his lips.

'Don't cry,' he said. 'I cannot let you leave me. I promise you that if you leave me, I shall die. But listen to me – I have a plan. Don't expect me here tomorrow.'

'Why not?' Cosette said, drying her tears. 'A whole day without seeing you! That's unbearable!'

'It's worth losing a day together if we want to be happy for the rest of our lives.'

'But what are you going to do?'

'Wait until the day after tomorrow. I'll tell you then. But until then, I must give you my address. I'm living with a friend of mine, Enjolras.' Marius then took a knife out of his pocket and scratched his address on the wall – 16, rue de la Verrerie.'

'Please, Marius,' Cosette said as she watched him. 'Where are you going tomorrow evening? I won't be able to sleep if you don't tell me.'

'I'm going to try something.'

'Well, I'll pray for you to succeed and I'll never stop thinking about you. I'll ask no more questions, but you must promise to be here early the day after tomorrow. Not later than nine o'clock.'

'I promise,' Marius said.

Chapter 9   Monsieur Gillenormand

M. Gillenormand, Marius's grandfather, was now ninety years old. He was unhappy about many things – about losing his teeth, about the political situation but, most of all, about the fact that he had not seen his grandson for four years, since their big quarrel. Although he was too proud to admit he was wrong, and although he was angry, M. Gillenormand hoped that Marius, whom he still loved, would return one day.

One evening in June, M. Gillenormand was sitting in front of a large fire, staring into the flames and thinking bitterly of Marius. He was feeling depressed, because he realized that he would probably never see his grandson again. While he was gazing into the fire, thinking these sad thoughts, his old servant entered the room and asked, 'Will Monsieur receive M. Marius?'

For a moment all the blood seemed to leave M. Gillenormand's face, and the servant began to worry that his master was ill. But the old man finally raised his head and said, in a low voice, 'Show him in.'

Marius stood uncertainly in the doorway. The poor condition of his clothes could not be seen in the half-darkness of the room. Nothing of him was clearly visible except his face, which was calm and serious, but strangely sad.

M. Gillenormand stared at his grandson with disbelief. At last! After four years! Was it really him? He wanted to open his arms and hug him, but all he said was, 'What have you come for?'

Marius murmured something in embarrassment.

'I can't hear you,' the old man said, looking annoyed. 'Have you come to apologize? Do you now see that you were wrong?'

'No, Monsieur.' Marius lowered his eyes.

'Well then,' the old man shouted, 'what do you want?'

'Monsieur, I ask you to have pity on me. I know I'm not welcome here, but I have come to ask for only one thing. Then I'll go away at once.'

'You're a young fool,' the old man said. 'Who said you had to go away? You left me – your grandfather! – to join in those street protests against the government, I suppose. You're probably in trouble with the police, or you're in debt, and you've run back to me for help . . .'

'Monsieur, it's none of those things.'

'Well, what is it exactly that you want?'

'I have come to ask your permission to get married.'

The old man paused for a moment before saying, 'So, you want to get married at the age of twenty-one. I suppose you've got some sort of career, now? Perhaps you've made a fortune. What do you earn as a lawyer?'

'Nothing.'

'Well then, I imagine the lucky girl must have money.'

'She's no richer than I am.'

'What does her father do?'

'I don't know.'

M. Gillenormand turned away with disgust.

'So that's it. Twenty-one years old, no job, no money. Your wife will have to count the sous when she goes to the market, won't she?'

'I beg you, Monsieur,' Marius cried. 'I love her so much. Please allow me to marry her!'

The old man gave a high, unpleasant laugh.

'So you said to yourself, "I'll have to go and see him, that old fool. He'll be so happy to see me that he won't care who I marry. I haven't a pair of shoes, and she hasn't a shirt, but never mind. I'm going to throw away my youth, my career, my whole life, and dive into poverty with a woman around my neck ..." That's what you think, isn't it? Well, my boy, you can do whatever you want. But I will never give you my permission! Never!'

'Grandfather ...'

'Never!'

The tone of his grandfather's voice robbed Marius of all hope. He rose and crossed the room slowly, with his head bowed. He had just reached the door, however, when M. Gillenormand moved quickly towards him, pulled him back into the room and pushed him into an armchair.

'Tell me about it,' he said to Marius, who stared back with silent amazement, unaware that the word 'grandfather' was responsible for the change in the old man's behaviour. 'Come on, tell me about your love affairs. Don't be afraid to talk. Don't forget, I'm your grandfather. Here ...' he said, taking a purse from a drawer and putting it on the table. 'Here's some money for you. Buy yourself some new clothes.'

Marius told his grandfather all about Cosette and how much he loved her. M. Gillenormand listened carefully and, when Marius had finished, he laughed.

'You must enjoy yourself when you're young,' he said. 'But you must also be sensible. Don't get married yet, that's my advice. Have fun with the girl, but don't marry her. Make her your lover but not your wife.'

Marius, too shocked to reply, shook his head and rose to his feet. He then turned slowly to the old man, bowed deeply and said, 'Four years ago you insulted my father. Today you have insulted my future wife. I shall ask no more favours of you, Monsieur. Goodbye.'

M. Gillenormand called for Marius to come back, but it was too late. The proud young man had closed the door and gone.

'Oh my God,' the old man cried, burying his face in his hands. 'What have I done? This time he'll never come back.'

♦

Marius left his grandfather's house in a state of despair, and returning to his room, fell asleep fully-dressed on the bed. When he woke up, Enjolras was in the room with a few other friends. They all looked very nervous and excited about something.

'What's the matter?' Marius asked sleepily.

'Are you coming to the funeral of General Lamarque?'

'Who's he?'

Enjolras and his friends shook their heads with amazement at their friend's lack of awareness, and soon left the room. Marius opened a drawer and took out the two guns which Inspector Javert had lent him in February. Putting them in his jacket pocket, he went out and continued to wander aimlessly around the streets, noticing only occasionally the strange atmosphere of excitement that was growing in the town. People were running around, and there was a lot of noise, but Marius paid little attention. He could think of only one thing: his meeting later that evening with Cosette. This would be his last brief happiness; after that, there would be only darkness.

At nine o'clock that evening, Marius crept into the garden of Cosette's house, but she was not there waiting for him as she had promised. Looking up, he saw that there were no lights on in the house and that all the windows were closed. Unable to control himself, he beat his fists against the walls of the house.

'Cosette!' he cried, not caring who heard him. 'Where are you?'

He called her name again and again until, exhausted, he sat down on the stone steps. Now she was gone, he told himself, he had no future. There was nothing for him to do except die.

Suddenly he heard a voice calling through the trees from the street.

'M. Marius!'

61

He looked up.

'Who's that?'

'Is that you, M. Marius?'

'Yes.'

'Your friends are waiting for you at the barricade in the rue de Chanvrerie.'

Marius ran to the gate and was just in time to see the figure of Éponine, Thénardier's daughter, disappearing into the shadows at the end of the street.

Chapter 10   The Barricade

In the spring of 1832, the people of Paris were ready for revolution. Charles X, who had become king in 1824, believed that he had total power over the French people. He was a strong supporter of the Catholic church and the aristocracy, and he took away the freedoms that Napoleon had given the ordinary citizens. Although this made him very unpopular, he thought that his opponents would be too weak to prevent him from doing what he wanted. He was wrong. In 1830, there was a peaceful revolution, and he was forced to leave. The new king, Louis-Philippe, was a brave and clever man who loved his country. The ordinary people liked him at first, but he soon showed that he was more interested in power for his family than democracy for his people. He understood business, but he could not understand the problems of poor people. Neither could he understand the concept of freedom of speech, and he often sent soldiers into the streets to attack people who were making public protests.

As the summer approached, the mood of the workers and the poor became angrier and angrier. Their anger exploded into violence in June 1832, when General Lamarque died. The

General had been very popular with the people of France because of his love for Napoleon. The day of his funeral was arranged for 5 June, and thousands of people saw this as a chance to make a public protest against the king and his government.

At first, the funeral went quietly. Soldiers accompanied the coffin as it was carried slowly across Paris. A large crowd followed behind, waving flags and carrying swords and heavy sticks. The crowd grew more and more excited, until finally they tried to take the coffin away from the soldiers and carry it across a bridge. Their exit was blocked by more soldiers on horseback. For a moment, nothing happened. Then there were two gunshots. The first shot killed the commander of the soldiers guarding the exit to the bridge. The second killed a deaf old woman who was trying to shut her window.

Then the fighting started.

Soldiers attacked the crowd with swords; the crowd threw stones and ran screaming across the bridge. Minutes later, the sounds of war echoed across the whole city of Paris.

◆

As soon as the fighting started, Enjolras and several of his friends started to build a barricade outside the Corinth wine shop in the rue de la Chanvrerie, a small street surrounded by dark alleys in the market district of Paris. Enjolras had been joined by many strangers as he and his friends had run shouting along the street. There was a tall, grey-haired man whom nobody knew, but whose strong, brave face had impressed everybody. There were several street children, excited by the sound of battle, who also joined them. One of these children was Éponine, who had dressed like a boy so that no one would tell her to go home. Having run to tell Marius that his friends were waiting for him, she was helping Enjolras and his companions to build the barricade. New people arrived all the time, bringing with them

63

gunpowder and weapons to fight the soldiers who would be arriving very soon.

Enjolras, who was the leader of the rebels, organized the building of a second barricade and the manufacture of bullets from melted silver. The tall, grey-haired man was doing useful work on the larger barricade, and Éponine (whom everyone thought was a boy) worked hard too. The barricades were finished in less than an hour and, with the sound of drums in the city growing louder, Enjolras brought a table out into the street and sat down with his friends for a drink.

Night fell, but nothing happened. While the fifty men behind the barricade waited impatiently for the arrival of sixty thousand soldiers, Enjolras approached the tall, grey-haired man.

'Who are you?' he asked.

When the man said nothing, Enjolras became suspicious.

'You're a policeman, aren't you?' he said.

The man smiled and eventually admitted that he was.

'My name's Javert,' he said.

Before he could move, Enjolras ordered four men to search him. When they found a letter in his pocket which proved that he had been sent to spy on them, they tied him to a post inside the inn.

'You'll be shot two minutes before the barricade falls,' Enjolras informed him.

◆

Marius left the garden and, mad with grief at losing Cosette, walked towards the sound of drums and gunfire in the centre of the city. He had only one thought in his mind: he wanted to die.

Marius pushed his way through the crowds of frightened, murmuring people that filled the streets until he reached the market area. Here, he found the unlit streets suddenly filled with soldiers. Unafraid, Marius ran through the shadows, ignoring shouts for him to stop. Someone fired a gun and a bullet hit a wall just behind him, but he didn't care.

He was just approaching the rue de Chanvrerie when he heard a loud voice calling from the shadows: 'Who's there?'

'The French Revolution!' he heard a distant voice reply – the voice of his friend, Enjolras.

Marius stood behind an alley wall, hidden in the shadows. Around the corner, he could see a row of soldiers aiming their guns down the rue de Chanvrerie, waiting for the order to fire.

'Fire!' the order finally came. The street was lit with a sudden flash of light and filled with the thunder of gunfire.

Then the soldiers attacked.

Marius stood up and ran along a series of alleys that led into the rue de la Chanvrerie, behind the Corinth wine shop. When he reached the stronghold, soldiers were already climbing the barricade, shooting at the rebels. Marius saw a soldier attacking Enjolras, who had fallen backwards and was calling for help. Marius took Javert's guns from his pockets and shot the soldier dead.

Soldiers now occupied the top of the barricade, but were unable to advance any further because the defenders fought so fiercely. Marius, who had thrown away his guns and was now without a weapon, began to move towards a barrel of gunpowder he had seen near the door of the wine shop. He did not notice a soldier aiming his gun at him. Neither did he see, at the moment the soldier fired, a young boy dressed in rags jump in front of the gun and fall wounded as the bullet meant for Marius hit him in the hand.

'Put down your weapons and surrender!' a soldier called from the top of the barricade.

'Fire!' Enjolras shouted.

The soldiers and the rebels fired at each other at the same time, filling the air with thick clouds of dark smoke. When the smoke cleared, there were many dead bodies on both sides. The survivors were reloading their guns in silence, when suddenly a loud voice called, 'Get out now, or I'll blow up the barricade!'

All heads turned to stare in the direction of the voice. Marius was standing at the foot of the barricade, holding a flaming torch above a barrel of gunpowder.

'If you blow up the barricade,' a sergeant called, 'you'll blow up yourself as well!'

Marius smiled and lowered the torch towards the gunpowder. Within seconds, the soldiers had left the barricade, leaving their dead and wounded behind, and were running into the darkness at the far end of the street.

Enjolras threw his arms around Marius's neck.

'So you've come!' he cried.

Marius hugged Enjolras and many other friends he recognized.

While the soldiers waited at the far end of the street for further orders, and the rebels removed dead bodies from the barricade and took care of the wounded, Marius walked around the stronghold in a kind of dream. After two months of happiness with Cosette, he was now in the middle of a war. He could not believe this was happening to him. He was so confused that he did not recognize Javert, tied to a post inside the inn throughout the battle.

As he was walking by the smaller barricade, his thoughts were interrupted by a weak voice calling his name from the shadows.

'M. Marius!'

He looked about him but, seeing no one, he started to walk away, thinking that he was imagining things.

'M. Marius!' He heard the voice again.

Marius gazed into the shadows, but could still see nothing.

'I'm at your feet,' the voice said.

Looking down, Marius saw a dark shape crawling along the

ground towards him. By the light of a lamp on the pavement, he could see a torn jacket, trousers with holes in them, and two bare feet. A white face was turned towards him and the voice asked, 'Do you recognize me? It's Éponine.'

Marius bent down quickly, and saw that it was indeed that unhappy girl, dressed in a man's clothes.

'What are you doing here?' he said. Then, noticing the pool of blood on the ground behind her, cried, 'You're wounded! I'll carry you to the inn. They'll take care of you there. Is it very bad?'

She showed him the bullet hole in her hand.

'A soldier was going to shoot you,' she said, her voice no more than a whisper. 'But I put my hand in front of his gun.'

'You poor child,' Marius said. 'We'll put a bandage on that wound immediately. You'll be all right.'

'The bullet passed through my hand,' Éponine murmured, 'but it came out through my back. It's no use trying to move me, but I'll tell you how you can treat my wound better than any doctor. Sit down on that stone, close beside me.'

Marius sat next to her. She rested her head on his knee and said without looking at him, 'Oh, what happiness. Now I don't feel any pain.'

For a moment she was silent. She pressed her hand to her chest, from which blood was pouring like dark wine. Then, with a great effort, she raised herself on one arm and, struggling for breath, looked into Marius's eyes.

'I can't cheat you,' she said at last. 'I have a letter for you in my pocket. I've had it since yesterday. I was asked to post it, but I didn't. I didn't want you to get it. But now we're both going to die, it doesn't matter, does it? I can't be jealous any more. Take your letter.'

She took hold of Marius's hand with her wounded hand and, without seeming to feel the pain, guided it to her pocket, from which he took the letter.

67

'Now you must promise me something for my trouble,' she said. 'You must kiss me on the forehead after I'm dead ... I shall know.'

She let her head fall back on his knees. Her eyelids trembled, and then she was still. Just as Marius thought that her sad soul had finally left her body, she slowly opened her eyes, and said in a voice so sweet that it seemed already to come from another world, 'You know, M. Marius, I think I was a little bit in love with you.'

With those words, she closed her eyes for the last time and died.

Marius kissed her pale forehead and laid her gently on the ground. Then he returned to the wine shop, and opened the letter that she had given him. By candlelight he read,

My dearest, We are leaving this house at once. We go tonight to Number 7, rue de l'Homme-Armé, and in a week we shall be in England. Cosette, 4 June.

Marius covered Cosette's letter with kisses. So she still loved him! He thought for a moment that now he must not die, but then he thought, 'She's going away.'

She was going with her father to England, and his grandfather had refused to give his permission for him to marry. Nothing had changed, and he decided that he had one last duty to perform: he must send Cosette a final message and tell her of his death. He tore a page out of the pocket notebook he always carried and wrote:

Our marriage was impossible. I went to my grandfather, and he refused to give his permission. I have no money, and neither have you. I hurried to see you, but you had gone. You remember the promise I made you. I shall keep it. I shall die. I love you. When you read this, my soul will be very near and smiling at you.

He folded the letter, wrote Cosette's new address on the back and called over a young boy.

'What's your name?' he asked the boy.

'Gavroche.'

'Well, Gavroche, will you do something for me? I want you to deliver this letter to the address written on the outside.'

The boy scratched his head, thought for a moment, and then, with a sudden movement, took the letter and ran off into the night.

Chapter 11   The Letter

Jean Valjean, at that moment, was in a state of terrible shock. For the first time in their life together, he and Cosette had quarrelled. She had not wanted to leave the house, but she had eventually obeyed him. They had left quickly, at nightfall, bringing their servant, Toussaint, with them, but very little luggage. Cosette had brought her letter case and blotter with her, Valjean his box of child's clothing and the old National Guard uniform which all respectable men possessed, and which he had worn under a previous identity.

In their new house, they went to bed in silence. Cosette, however, did not leave her bedroom the next day, and Jean Valjean had dinner alone. As he was eating, Toussaint told him about the fighting in the city, but he did not pay much attention. He was too worried about Cosette. There was no reason, he thought, why they should not continue to live happily together in England. As long as he had Cosette, he would be happy, and it did not matter where they lived. He began to feel happier as he thought about the journey they would soon be making. He stood up and was going to leave the room when something made him stop. He glanced again at the mirror. Cosette's blotter was lying on a cupboard just below it and, as Valjean stared at its reflection, he read the following lines:

My dearest, We are leaving this house at once. We go tonight to Number 7, rue de l'Homme-Armé, and in a week we shall be in England. Cosette, 4 June.

In her unhappy state of mind, Cosette had forgotten to remove the page that she had used to blot the letter she had written to Marius. She had left it on the cupboard and the mirror, reflecting the backwards handwriting, made the message clearly visible.

Valjean moved closer to the mirror and read the lines again, not wanting to believe them. But there was no doubt that this was Cosette's handwriting. He began to shake and he fell back into an armchair, feeling angry and betrayed. He had suffered terribly over the years and, until now, he had survived every disaster. But this was the worst thing that had ever happened to him – someone was threatening to rob him of the only person he loved!

He murmured to himself, 'She's going to leave me,' and the pain of those words cut into his heart like a knife.

After a short time, he rose to his feet and looked again at the blotter. His anger and misery of minutes before had been replaced by a terrible calmness. He stared at the blotter, coldness in his eyes, the darkness of the deepest night in his heart. He remembered clearly the young man in the Luxembourg Gardens who had shown such great interest in Cosette, and he was certain that this was the man she had written to.

He went out into the night and sat on the doorstep, his heart filled with a terrible hatred for the man who was trying to steal Cosette from him. He sat for a long time listening to the sound of distant gunfire in the city, wondering how to get his revenge, when suddenly he heard footsteps. Looking up, he saw a pale-faced boy, dressed in rags, studying the numbers of the houses in the street.

Seeing Valjean on his doorstep, the boy stopped and asked, 'Do you live in this street?'

'Yes. Why?'

'I'm looking for Number Seven. I have a letter for a girl who lives here.'

'Well, I'm the girl's father. You can give the letter to me. Oh, and one more thing before you go,' Valjean said when the boy had handed him the letter. 'Where should I take the reply?'

'That letter comes from the barricade in the rue de la Chanvrerie,' the boy replied. 'Which is where I'm going now. Goodnight citizen.'

Jean Valjean went back into the house and tried to make sense of the words that danced before his eyes: *I shall die . . . When you read this, my soul will be very near . . .*

This was enough to fill his hate-filled heart with sudden joy. So, the problem was solved! The man who threatened his happiness was going to die – was perhaps already dead.

Then Valjean frowned and, after a quick calculation, decided that Marius was probably still alive. But it made no difference. He was still certain to die, and Valjean's happiness would be safe. If he kept the letter in his pocket, Cosette would never know what had happened to the other man, and life with her would continue the same as before. What happiness!

But his happiness had no sooner returned than it disappeared again in a cloud of despair. In his heart he knew he had no choice. For the sake of Cosette's happiness, he would have to try and save the life of the man she loved – the man he hated more than any other in the world.

Half an hour later he left the house, dressed in his National Guard uniform, with a loaded gun and a pocket full of gunpowder, and made his way towards the market district of Paris.

Chapter 12   Fight to the Death

During the night, the thirty-seven remaining rebels strengthened the main barricade and made more bullets. The ground floor of the wine shop became a hospital for the wounded, and the bodies of the dead were taken to an alley near the smaller of the two barricades. Four of the dead people were National Guards, and their uniforms were removed.

After a long discussion with his friends, Enjolras decided that the married men (there were five of them) had to leave.

'It's your duty not to die,' he told them. 'You must return to your families.'

'How can we leave?' they protested. 'We're surrounded. The soldiers will shoot us as soon as they see us.'

'You can wear these.' Enjolras pointed to the National Guard uniforms that had been taken off the dead soldiers.

'But there are only four,' Marius observed.

'Then one of us must stay and fight,' one of the married men replied.

A long argument followed, during which each of the married men tried to persuade the others to go. Finally, someone shouted to Marius, 'You decide which one must stay.'

Marius went pale at the thought of having to choose which man had to die. He stared down at the four uniforms but, as he did so, a fifth uniform fell as if by magic at his feet.

Looking round, Marius recognized Cosette's father. Jean Valjean, who had arrived unnoticed at the barricade, had been listening to the argument and had quickly understood the situation.

'Now you can all leave,' he said.

The sky grew lighter, but not a door or window was open in the street. The barricade was stronger than it had been for the first assault, and the rebels were at their positions, guns loaded and ready for action. They did not have long to wait.

Sounds of chains and of heavy wheels moving along the stone streets could be heard, and then soldiers came into view at the end of the street, pulling a large cannon. The rebels fired their guns but, when the smoke had cleared, they saw the soldiers, unharmed, steadily aiming the cannon at the barricade. Moments later, an officer shouted a command and the cannon roared into action. The cannonball crashed into the bottom of the barricade with a loud explosion, but did little damage. The rebels clapped and cheered.

More soldiers moved into position at the end of the street, behind the cannon, and started to build a low wall with pieces of broken stone. At the same time, the leader of the gun crew adjusted the aim of the cannon.

'Heads down!' Enjolras shouted.

The next cannonball exploded against the wall at one end of the barricade, killing two men and wounding three.

'We mustn't let that happen again,' Enjolras said. He aimed his gun over the barricade at the leader of the gun crew, and fired. The gunner – a fair-haired, handsome young man – spun round twice with his head thrown back, and fell sideways across the cannon. Blood poured from the middle of his back.

A tear rolled down Enjolras's cheek.

'It's sad,' he murmured to Marius, who was standing next to him. 'He looked a brave young man.'

♦

The battle continued for some time; the cannon destroyed the upper windows of the wine shop, and did some damage to the barricade, but the rebels did not withdraw. They fired back at the soldiers, killing many men. In the pauses between shooting, the rebels could hear the sound of fighting in other parts of Paris. They were filled with hope that help would come soon, but the hope did not last long. Within half an hour the sound of gunfire in other places had stopped, and the rebels knew that they were alone. When a second cannon was moved into position next to the first, they knew that the end was near.

Both cannons fired together, accompanied by gunfire from soldiers at the end of the street and on the rooftops. As other guns began firing at the smaller barricade, the rebels fought back bravely, but they were running out of bullets. There were only twenty-six men left, and the main attack on the barricade was going to take place very soon. Some men, including Marius, stayed on the main barricade, while the others built a low stone wall around the door of the wine shop. Enjolras, inside the wine shop, turned to Javert, who was still tied to the post.

'I haven't forgotten you,' he said, putting a loaded gun on the table. 'The last man to leave this place will blow your brains out.'

At this point, Jean Valjean spoke to Enjolras.

'You're the leader, aren't you? Can I ask you for a favour?'

'You saved a man's life by giving him your uniform. You deserve some reward. What do you want?'

'Let me kill this man.'

'That's fair,' Enjolras decided, when nobody objected. 'You can have your spy.'

At the same moment there was the sound of a drum, followed by a loud roar.

'They're coming!' cried Marius from the top of the barricade.

The rebels rushed to their positions, leaving Valjean alone with Javert inside the wine shop. Valjean untied the rope around Javert's feet and, taking him by the belt of his coat, led him outside. Only Marius, looking over his shoulder, saw them cross the stronghold towards the smaller barricade. Valjean, his gun in one hand, pulled Javert behind him over the barricade and into a narrow alley, where the corner of a house hid them from view. A terrible heap of dead bodies lay not far away, among them the blood-stained body of a young girl in man's clothes – Éponine.

Javert glanced at the dead body and murmured, 'I think I know that girl.' Then, returning his attention to Valjean, he said calmly, 'I think you know me, too. Take your revenge.'

Valjean, however, took a knife from his pocket and cut the ropes that tied Javert's wrists.

'You're free to go,' he said.

When Javert stared at him, speechless with surprise, Valjean went on, 'I don't suppose I'll leave here alive. But if I do, I'm staying at Number 7, rue de l'Homme-Armé. Now go.'

Javert buttoned his coat, straightened his shoulders and, with a puzzled look on his face, began to walk off in the direction of the market. He had only gone a few steps, however, when he turned and looked at Valjean. 'I find this embarrassing,' he said. 'I'd rather you killed me.'

'Go away,' Valjean replied.

Javert walked away slowly and Valjean, waiting for him to turn a corner, fired his gun into the air and returned to the stronghold.

'It's done,' he said.

◆

There was a roar of gunfire and the soldiers attacked, rushing towards the barricade. Many fell, but many more reached the barricade. The first assault was beaten back by the brave rebels, but the soldiers attacked again and again. Soon, the ground below the barricade was piled with dead and wounded men as the rebels and soldiers fought hand to hand. The rebels fought long and hard to defend the stronghold, but finally they had to withdraw to the low wall outside the wine shop. They stood with their backs to the door, shooting up at the soldiers who were climbing down towards them from the barricade. One by one the remaining rebels escaped into the wine shop, until only Enjolras and Marius were left outside. As the two friends moved back towards the door, fighting off the soldiers, a bullet hit

Marius in the shoulder. His eyes closed and, in great pain, he felt a hand grab him as he fell.

'They've taken me prisoner,' he thought, moments before losing consciousness. 'Now I shall be shot.'

The soldiers, meanwhile, attacked the wine shop. Before long, they broke down the door and rushed inside. Enjolras and the few surviving rebels fought bravely, but the soldiers were too strong. Soon, all the rebels were dead, including Enjolras, who was the last to die. Sword in hand, surrounded by soldiers, he refused to surrender. He died in a rain of bullets with a strangely victorious smile on his lips.

Chapter 13   The Sewers of Paris

Marius had indeed been taken prisoner, but not by the soldiers. It was Jean Valjean's hand that had caught him as he fell. Valjean had taken no part in the battle. He had been looking after wounded men while bullets flew all around him. When Marius had been hit, Valjean ran to him at once, grabbed him before he fell and carried his unconscious body into a small alley behind the wine shop. Valjean lowered Marius to the ground, stood with his back to the wall and looked around him.

The situation was terrible. There seemed to be no escape. On one side of him was the field of battle. On the other side was the low barricade, behind which hundreds of soldiers waited for rebels trying to escape. Both ways meant certain death. It was a situation that only a bird could have escaped from. Valjean looked desperately around him, at the house opposite, the barricade, the ground. And then he had a sudden idea!

At the foot of the smaller barricade, half-hidden by broken stones and pieces of wood, there was a hole in the road covered with an iron grille. Valjean leapt forward and, using all his strength, he moved the stones and wood, opened the grille, lifted Marius on to his shoulders and climbed down into the darkness.

A few minutes later, he found himself in a long underground passage, a place of absolute peace and silence. He was inside the Paris sewers. He could just see, by the grey light from the grille above his head, that he was surrounded by walls. Ahead of him lay total darkness, but he had to go on. The soldiers might discover the grille by the barricade at any moment, and come down in search of him.

With Marius lying across his shoulders, Valjean walked forward into the darkness, feeling his way along the wet, slippery walls with his hands. He moved from one passage into another, slipping several times on the wet floor. He could not see where he was going, but he knew he had to follow the downward slope of the passages towards the river.

He walked blindly downwards in this way for a long time, his clothes wet with the blood from Marius's wound, the faint whisper of the young man's breath in his ear. He walked in total darkness, the silence broken occasionally by the thunder of gun carriages and horses racing along the streets of Paris far above his head.

Suddenly, he saw his own shadow on the floor of the passage in front of him. Looking back, he saw the distant light of a torch. He was being followed! He pressed himself against the wall, held his breath and waited. In the distance, a group of men formed a circle around the torchlight. They seemed to be listening for something, waiting for someone to move. Finally, the group of men moved off along another passage, and Valjean was left in total darkness once again.

He continued his journey through the sewers. Sometimes the roof of the passages was so low that he had to bend down as he walked. His feet slipped all the time in the water on the ground, and he felt sick and faint with the terrible, airless smell. At last, exhausted, he stopped beneath a large grille that brought him much-needed light and fresh air. He laid Marius down gently at the edge of the sewer, and looked down at his face. It was covered with blood and as pale as death. Valjean tore pieces off his own shirt and bandaged Marius's wounded shoulder as well as he could. Then, bending over the unconscious body, Valjean stared at Marius with hatred in his eyes.

He found two objects in Marius's clothing: a piece of bread and a wallet. Valjean ate the bread and, opening the wallet, found a note which Marius had written:

> My name is Marius Pontmercy. My body must be taken to the house of my grandfather, M. Gillenormand, 6 rue des Filles-du-Calvaire, in the Marais.

Valjean repeated the address until he could remember it, returned the wallet to Marius's pocket, picked Marius up again and continued his journey downwards towards the river. He did not know what part of the city he was passing under or how far he had come. The only thing he was sure of was that the light through the grilles far above his head was growing weaker, which meant that the sun was setting. At one point he had to walk waist-deep through water, and almost sank as the ground turned to sand beneath his feet. Finally, when even his great strength was beginning to fade, he saw ahead of him a light – the clear light of day. He was suddenly filled with new energy at the sight, at last, of his way of escape from the sewers. Forgetting the weight of Marius on his shoulders and his own hunger and tiredness, he ran towards the light. He had to bend as the roof of the tunnel became lower, but when he reached the light, Valjean stopped and gave a cry of despair. The opening was closed with a strong iron gate, held firm by a huge, rusty lock. Through the bars, Valjean could see daylight, the river, a narrow riverbank – but how could he get out?

Valjean laid Marius down by the wall, where the floor was dry. Then, moving to the gate, he shook it fiercely with both hands, trying to bend the bars with the last of his strength. But the gate was solid and the bars were firm.

Valjean turned his back to the gate and sank to the ground, his head bowed between his knees. There was no way out and, as all hope of escape left him, he began to think of Cosette.

◆

While in this state of despair, Valjean felt a hand on his shoulder. He thought he was dreaming. He looked up and saw a man dressed in old clothes standing beside him. Despite the unexpectedness of this meeting, Valjean recognized the man at once. It was Thénardier. Valjean did not show that he recognized the man, and saw with relief that Thénardier had not recognized *him*.

'I'll make a bargain with you,' the man said.

'What do you mean?'

Thénardier nodded in Marius's direction.

'You've killed a man. Give me half of what you found in this man's pockets, and I'll unlock the gate for you.' He produced a large key from his pocket, and a piece of rope. 'I'll give you this as well,' he said. 'Then you can tie stones to the body and throw it in the river.'

Valjean took the rope without speaking.

'What about my share of the money?' Thénardier asked.

Valjean took thirty francs from his pockets and showed it to Thénardier, who stared with disbelief. 'You killed a man for just thirty francs? You're a fool.' He searched Marius's pockets himself, and then Valjean's.

'It's true,' he said at last. 'That's all there is. Oh well. Never say that I'm not a kind man.'

He took the thirty francs and, helping Valjean to lift Marius on to his shoulders, he put the key in the lock and opened the gate just wide enough for Valjean to pass through. When Valjean was outside, Thénardier closed the gate behind him and disappeared, like a rat, into the darkness of the sewers.

◆

Valjean laid Marius gently on the grass and stood up, surrounded by silence, enjoying the feeling of fresh air on his face. Then, just as he was bending to splash water from the river on Marius's face, he was aware of someone else standing behind him. He looked round quickly and saw a tall man in a long coat, a large stick in his hand. Although the man's face was hidden in shadow, Valjean recognized him as Inspector Javert.

Javert, however, did not recognize Valjean at first. He had been more interested in catching Thénardier, who had escaped from prison and was known to be in the area.

'Who are you?' he asked.

Valjean told him his name and stood, without moving, as Javert approached and stared into his eyes.

'Inspector Javert,' Valjean said quietly. 'I beg you to do me one favour. I promise not to try and escape. I gave you my address this morning, if you remember, so you would know where to find me anyway.'

Javert did not seem to hear. He stared into Valjean's eyes for a long time, then, stepping back with a look of confusion in his eyes, asked dreamily, 'What are you doing here? Who is this man?'

'Will you help me to take him home?' Valjean said. 'He's badly injured.'

Javert looked unhappy, but he did not refuse. Bending down, he took a handkerchief from his pocket, wet it in the river and bathed Marius's blood-stained forehead. Then he felt Marius's wrist.

'He's dead,' he said.

'No, not yet,' Valjean replied, feeling in Marius's jacket for the wallet. 'Look,' he said, showing Javert the note with Marius's grandfather's address. 'That's where we need to take him.'

Javert shouted to the driver who was waiting for him to bring his carriage close to the river. With Marius in the back seat, Valjean and Javert side by side in the front, the carriage drove off quickly through the dark and strangely empty streets of Paris.

When they arrived at M. Gillenormand's house, a servant answered the door.

'Does M. Gillenormand live here?' Javert asked.

'Yes. What do you want?'

'We're bringing back his grandson. He's dead. Go and wake his grandfather. We're bringing him in.'

Javert, Valjean and the driver carried Marius into the house and laid him gently on a sofa in M. Gillenormand's sitting-room. While one servant ran to find a doctor and another looked for clean sheets, Valjean felt Javert's hand on his arm. He understood, and went downstairs with Javert close behind him. When they had got back into the carriage, however, Valjean said, 'Inspector, will you do one last thing for me before you arrest me?'

'What is it?' Javert replied impatiently.

'Let me go home for a minute. After that, you can do whatever you want with me.'

Javert was silent for some moments, his chin sunk in the collar of his overcoat. Then he pulled down the window in front of him.

'Number 7, rue de l'Homme-Armé,' he told the driver.

Neither man spoke during the journey. At the end of the rue de l'Homme-Armé, which was too narrow for the carriage to enter, Javert paid the driver and accompanied Valjean to his front door on foot.

'Go in,' said Javert, with a strange, distant look in his eyes. 'I'll wait for you here.'

Valjean went into his house and called, 'It's me!' Climbing the stairs, he paused for a moment to look out of the window to see what Javert was doing. But the street was empty; there was no one there.

The next morning, Inspector Javert's body was discovered floating in the river. The poor man, unable to understand the kindness and gentle nature of the man he had spent his whole life hating, had taken his own life by jumping from a bridge. It was the only way he knew to escape the confusion that was poisoning his heart.

◆

When M. Gillenormand saw his pale, lifeless-looking grandson lying on the sofa, he shook from head to foot. Leaning against the door for support, he murmured, 'Marius!'

'He has just been brought here,' said a servant. 'He was on the barricade and . . .'

'He's dead!' cried the old man in a terrible voice. 'The fool! He did this to hurt me, the ungrateful boy. I try to be good to him, and this is how he rewards me!'

The old man walked to the window and, while he complained to the night about the pain and grief his grandson had caused him, the doctor arrived. After listening to Marius's heart, he organized his removal to a bed in another room, and returned to M. Gillenormand, who was still standing by the window.

'Will he live?' M. Gillenormand asked, his eyes wild with fear.

'I don't know,' the doctor replied. 'The wound to his body is not serious, but there are deep cuts on his head. It's difficult to say . . .'

M. Gillenormand went to Marius's bedside.

'You heartless boy,' he said angrily. 'A fool who prefers fighting to dancing and having fun. What kind of man are you? Are you mad? But it makes no difference. I too shall die. That makes you a murderer, a cold-hearted killer. I cannot feel grief for you . . .'

At that moment, Marius's eyes slowly opened and his gaze rested upon M. Gillenormand.

'Marius!' the old man cried. 'Marius, my child, grandson! You're alive after all!'

Chapter 14   The Wedding

Marius lay for a long time between life and death in a state of fever, endlessly repeating the name of Cosette.

'He mustn't get excited,' the doctor warned.

Every day, according to one of the servants, a white-haired, well-dressed gentleman came to ask for news of the sick man.

Finally, after three months, the doctor announced that Marius was out of danger. But he had to spend the next two months resting because of the damage to his shoulder. M Gillenormand grew happier as his grandson's condition improved. He did strange, unexpected things, like running up and down stairs without knowing why. He gave his neighbour, a pretty woman, a bunch of flowers, which greatly annoyed her husband.

Marius, meanwhile, tried to make sense of what had happened to him. He thought about Enjolras and Éponine, and wondered why Cosette's father had been at the barricade. He could not understand why nobody could tell him how he had been saved. All he knew was that he had been brought to his grandfather's house in a carriage. He noticed his grandfather's tenderness towards him, but he could not forget the old man's unfairness and cruelty to his father, who had died penniless and unloved. Most of all, however, he thought about Cosette, and how he could find her again.

'There's something I have to say to you,' Marius told his grandfather one day.

'What is it?'

'I want to get married.'

'But of course,' the old man laughed.

'What do you mean – of course?'

'That's understood. You will have your little girl.'

'I don't understand,' Marius said, almost speechless with amazement.

'You will have her,' the old man repeated. 'She comes here every day in the shape of an old man who asks for news of you. While you've been ill, she's spent her time crying and making bandages for you. I know all about her. She lives at Number 7, rue de l'Homme-Armé. You see, I'm not as unkind as you think. I've found out that she's a charming girl and that she loves you. I knew you were angry with me, and I thought, "What can I do to make him love me?" Then I thought, "I can give him Cosette." I wanted to invite her to see you, but the doctor warned me that you would probably get too excited. So I advise you, dear boy, to eat more meat and get better soon. Then you can marry your Cosette and be happy.'

Having said this, the old man burst into tears. He held Marius's head to his chest and they cried together.

'Grandfather,' Marius said at last, 'I'm feeling much better already. When can I see her?'

'You can see her tomorrow.'

'Why not today?'

'All right, I'll fetch her today. You've called me "grandfather"; you've shown me that you love me after all. You've earned your reward!'

◆

Later that day, Cosette arrived at M. Gillenormand's house. Standing beside her on the doorstep was a white-haired man with a strangely nervous smile.

84

M. Gillenormand showed them up to the room where Marius was waiting. Cosette stood in the doorway, overcome with happiness. She wanted to throw herself into Marius's arms, but was unable to move, afraid to show the world that she loved him.

'Monsieur.' M. Gillenormand addressed Jean Valjean. 'I have the honour, on behalf of my grandson, Marius Pontmercy, to ask for your daughter's hand in marriage.'

Jean Valjean bowed.

'Good, then that is agreed,' M. Gillenormand said and, turning to Marius and Cosette, he added, 'My children, you are free to love one another.'

When they were alone together, Cosette and Marius kissed.

'Is it really you?' Cosette murmured at last. 'I can't believe it. I'm so happy to see you. I was so excited today that I haven't even dressed up for you. I must look terrible. But why don't you say something? Why are you letting me do all the talking? Do you still love me? Oh, I'm so wild with happiness . . .'

'My love . . .' Marius whispered.

◆

The wedding was arranged for February the following year. Jean Valjean arranged everything. Having been a mayor, he knew how to solve an awkward problem: the question of Cosette's real family. He told everybody that he was not her father, but her guardian. He also invented a dead family for Cosette, so that everybody believed she was an orphan. Valjean, as her guardian, gave Cosette a large amount of money – half a million francs – but did not tell her that the money was his. He told her that the money came from a man who preferred to remain unknown. It was arranged that the couple, who could not believe their sudden, new-found happiness, would live with M. Gillenormand after the wedding.

Cosette, accompanied by Jean Valjean, visited Marius every

day. Marius did not speak much to Valjean. Despite enjoying an occasional conversation with him, he found something strange about the old man. He could not believe that this was the same man he had seen at the barricade all those months ago – it seemed like a bad dream to him.

But there were more important things for Marius to think about. Apart from preparing for his wedding, there were two people that he wanted to find. First, there was Thénardier.

He was, without doubt, a bad man, but Marius had promised his father to find him and help him. He employed agents to find Thénardier, but without success. The only thing they discovered was that Mme Thénardier had died, and that her husband had escaped from prison and disappeared with his surviving daughter, Azelma.

Second, there was the mysterious stranger who had saved his life. Marius's attempts to find him also ended in failure, and the true story of his escape from the barricade remained a complete mystery to him.

One evening, when Marius was talking to Cosette and Jean Valjean about the mystery and his unsuccessful attempts to solve it, he became angry with Cosette's guardian's lack of interest in his story.

'The man was a hero,' Marius said. 'Do you realize, Monsieur, how brave this man was? He rescued me from the field of battle and carried me through the sewers of Paris. He risked his life to save a dying man, and why? He was a total stranger. He did it without any thought of a reward. Oh, I wish Cosette's money were mine.'

'It *is* yours,' Valjean reminded him.

'I would give it all,' said Marius, 'to find that man!'

Jean Valjean was silent.

♦

Cosette and Marius made a handsome couple on their wedding day. All previous unhappiness was forgotten as they kissed in the church, watched proudly by M. Gillenormand and Jean Valjean. There were flowers everywhere when they returned to M. Gillenormand's house for the wedding feast. It was the happiest night of Cosette's life, spoilt only by one thing: the fact that her guardian – whom she still thought of as her father – went home before the feast had started, saying that he felt ill. But Cosette was not unhappy for long. She had Marius, and she would be happy with him for the rest of her life!

Jean Valjean, meanwhile, went home, lit his candle and went upstairs to bed. That night, however, he was unable to sleep. He remembered the little girl he had rescued from the Thénardiers ten years earlier, and felt sad that he was no longer the most important man in her life. Another man was the centre of her universe. He was proud of having helped to bring her happiness with Marius, but another thing troubled his soul: the fact that nobody, not even Cosette, knew the truth about him. That he was Jean Valjean, a criminal who had spent nineteen years in prison and who had stolen silver candlesticks from a trusting and kind-hearted bishop. He knew that if he told Cosette and Marius the truth, he would spoil everybody's happiness and he would lose their love and respect. On the other hand, if he continued to lie about his past, he would lose his own soul. What could he do?

◆

The next day Valjean visited M. Gillenormand's house, and asked to speak to Marius in private. Marius hugged Valjean warmly, addressed him as 'father' and invited him to lunch, but Valjean shook his head and said, 'Monsieur, I have something to tell you.'

Marius listened quietly as Valjean told him everything about his life. Finally, in a state of shock and confusion, the young man said, 'Why have you told me all this? No one forced you to.'

'If I had continued to keep my secret to myself, I would have destroyed my own heart,' Valjean replied. 'Besides, I belong to no family. Cosette was the only family I ever had. Everything ended for me when she married you yesterday. She is happy with the man she loves. I tried to persuade myself that it would be better not to admit the truth about my past, but it was no use. I could not silence the voice that speaks to me when I am alone.'

Neither of them spoke for several minutes. Then Marius murmured, 'Poor Cosette. When she hears . . .'

'But you must promise not to tell her!' Valjean interrupted. 'She'll be heart-broken if she hears the truth about me. I don't think I could bear it . . .'

He sank into an armchair and buried his face in his hands.

'Don't worry,' Marius said at last. 'I'll keep your secret. But I think it would be better if you stopped seeing her.'

'I understand,' Valjean said, rising to leave. But at the door he half-turned and said, 'Monsieur, if you will permit me, I would like to come and see her. I wouldn't come often or stay very long. We could meet in that little room on the ground floor. Please Monsieur, if I can't see Cosette again, I'll have nothing left to live for. Besides, if I suddenly stopped visiting, people would become suspicious and begin to talk . . .'

'You can come every evening,' said Marius.

'Monsieur, you are very kind,' said Jean Valjean, shaking Marius's hand and leaving the room.

Chapter 15   The Truth at Last

Marius kept his promise about not telling Cosette, and Valjean visited her every evening in a small room on the ground floor. It was cold and damp, but a fire had been lit and two armchairs had

88

been placed in front of it. At first, Cosette could not understand why Valjean refused to meet her upstairs. When he refused to kiss her cheek, she began to feel unhappy, afraid that she had done something to offend him. She pressed his hands in hers and held them to her lips.

'Please, please be kind!' she begged. 'I want you to come and live with us. You'll always be my father and I'm not going to let you go.'

He released his hands.

'You mustn't call me "father" any more,' he told her. 'You must call me "Monsieur Jean".'

'I don't understand,' she said, becoming angry. 'This is ridiculous. You're upsetting me very much, and I don't know why you're being so cruel.'

'You don't need a father any more. You have a husband.'

'What a thing to say!' Cosette replied. 'Are you angry with me because I'm happy?'

'Cosette,' he said, 'your happiness is the only thing that matters to me. You're happy now, and so my work is complete.'

With these words, he picked up his hat and left.

Jean Valjean continued his evening visits, but the relationship between himself and Cosette became cooler and more distant. She stopped calling him 'father' or asking him questions. As 'Monsieur Jean', he gradually became a different person to her, and she began not to depend on him for her happiness.

Valjean would sit looking at Cosette in silence, or would talk about incidents from their past. One evening in April, he called at the usual time but was told that Cosette had gone out with her husband. He waited in the small, damp room for an hour before sadly returning home. Over the next few days, his visits began to be interrupted by servants calling Cosette to dinner. When he arrived, he discovered that the fire had not been lit, and the armchairs had been left near the door. One evening he discovered there were no chairs in the room at all – he and Cosette had to stand in the cold for their whole meeting. Valjean realized what was happening; Marius was telling the servants not to make him welcome any more. That night he went home in despair, and the next evening he did not come at all.

When Valjean did not appear for the second evening, Cosette sent a servant to his house to ask if he was well. Valjean replied that he was very well, but that he had business to attend to. He did not return to the house again, and Cosette was too busy with married life to think too much about him. She did not realize that, every evening, Valjean would walk slowly from his house until he reached the corner of the street where she lived. He would then stare at the house for several minutes, tears rolling down his cheeks, before turning round and slowly returning home.

♦

Marius thought it was right to exclude Valjean from Cosette's life. He achieved this without cruelty, but without weakness. Apart from the details about his life that Valjean had confessed to him, he knew that Valjean had killed Inspector Javert at the barricade. His private investigations into the old man's past had also revealed an even more disgusting fact. He had discovered that Valjean's money really belonged to somebody called Monsieur Madeleine, a wealthy manufacturer from Montreuil who had mysteriously disappeared. He persuaded Cosette, therefore, not to use any of the money her guardian had given her, and to live on the money that he had started to earn as a lawyer. Cosette had not been happy about this. She could not understand why her father, as she still thought of Valjean, had stopped visiting her. She still loved him in her heart. But she loved her husband even more, and she gradually became used to not depending on the old man for her happiness.

One evening a servant brought Marius a letter, saying, 'The writer is waiting in the hall.'

The smell of tobacco and the handwriting on the envelope was so familiar that Marius immediately thought of the Jondrettes. He read the letter quickly. It was signed 'Thenard', and was asking for money. Marius could not believe his luck. He had tried without success to find the man who had saved his father's life at Waterloo, and now the man had come to *him*! He immediately asked the servant to show the man in.

However, Marius had a shock when he saw the man – he did not recognize him at all! He was an old man with a big nose, glasses and neat grey hair. He was wearing smart black clothes, and a gold watch chain hung from his jacket pocket.

'What do you want?' Marius asked coldly, as the stranger bowed to him.

The stranger explained in great detail how he used to work for the government in foreign countries and that, now he was retired, he wanted to move to South America with his wife and daughter. Unfortunately, it was a long journey, and he needed money.

'What has that to do with me?'

'Has M. Pontmercy not read my letter?'

Marius had only read the letter quickly, and could not remember the details, so he said, 'Go on.'

'I have a secret to tell you, M. Pontmercy,' the stranger said. 'I'll tell you the first part for nothing. I think you'll be interested.'

'Well?'

'The man you think is your wife's guardian is a murderer and a thief. His name is Jean Valjean.'

'I know that.'

'Did you know that he spent nineteen years in prison?'

'I know that too.'

The stranger narrowed his eyes, trying to hide his

disappointment and anger at Marius's calmness. Then he gave a strange smile.

'I have more information to tell you. It concerns money that belongs to your wife. It's a remarkable secret and I'll sell the information to you for 20,000 francs.'

'I know this secret already,' Marius said, 'just as I knew the others.'

'10,000 francs?'

'I repeat, you have nothing to tell me.'

'But I need to eat, Monsieur!' the visitor said, losing confidence. 'I'll tell you for twenty francs.'

'I know it already,' Marius said. 'I know everything. I even know your real name. It's Thénardier.'

The visitor laughed, but Marius went on, 'You're also Jondrette. And you once had an inn in Montfermeil.'

'I deny it!'

'You're a completely rotten man, but I'll give you this.' Marius took a banknote out of his pocket and threw it in the stranger's face.

'Thank you, M. Pontmercy!' the man said, examining the note. '500 francs! That's real money. Oh well, I suppose we can relax.'

With those words, he removed his false nose, glasses and neat grey wig.

'M. Pontmercy is absolutely right,' he said, changing his voice. 'I am Thénardier.'

He waited for a few seconds to see Marius's reaction.

Marius, meanwhile, was grateful for finally having the chance to help Thénardier, and therefore to keep the promise he had made to his father. Thénardier's presence, however, offered him another opportunity; it gave him the chance to solve the mystery of Cosette's fortune.

'Thénardier,' he said. 'Shall I tell you the secret that you were planning to sell me? I, too, have sources of information, and probably know more about the subject than you do. Jean Valjean, as you say, is a murderer and a thief. He's a thief because he robbed a wealthy manufacturer and mayor of Montreuil, M. Madeleine. Jean Valjean, who knew the mayor's background, reported him to the police and took advantage of his arrest to take over half a million francs from his Paris bank. The manager of the bank told me this himself. And he murdered the policeman, Javert. I know this because I was there at the time.'

Thénardier looked puzzled for a moment, then said, 'Monsieur, I think you are mistaken.'

'What! Are you denying what I said? Those are facts!'

'They are incorrect, and I do not like to hear a man unjustly accused. Jean Valjean did not rob M. Madeleine, nor did he kill Javert.'

'How do you know?'

'First, he did not kill M. Madeleine because he *was* M. Madeleine! And second, he did not kill Javert because Javert killed himself. He killed himself by jumping into the river.'

'What proof do you have?' Marius said, wide-eyed with disbelief.

'I have all the proof here,' Thénardier said, producing an envelope in which there were several documents and newspaper articles. 'I've spent a long time discovering the truth about Jean Valjean.'

Marius studied the documents carefully, then looked up with a smile of joy. 'But he's a splendid man! The fortune was really his, and he's not a murderer or thief at all! He's a hero and a saint!'

'He's a thief and a murderer,' Thénardier said quietly.

'What do you mean?'

'I told you that I do not like to see a man accused unjustly, but I *do* like to see a man punished for crimes he *has* committed.'

'And what crimes are those?'

93

Thénardier sat down and told Marius about the time he had helped Valjean to escape from the Paris sewer.

'He was carrying the body of a man he had robbed and killed,' Thénardier said. 'Look, I have a piece of cloth from the dead man's coat as proof.'

He produced a muddy piece of cloth and showed it to Marius, who immediately went pale and rose unsteadily to his feet. As Thénardier continued to talk, Marius opened a cupboard door and took out a coat.

'That man was *me*!' Marius cried. 'And here is the coat I was wearing!'

Thénardier stared at the coat and the cloth in his hands, speechless with fear. He was even more surprised when, instead of chasing him out of the room, Marius ran towards him and pressed several thousand-franc notes into his hand.

'You're a terrible man,' Marius said. 'A thief and a liar. You came here to destroy a man, but you have done the opposite. If you hadn't saved my father's life at Waterloo, I'd report you to the police. I know that your wife is dead, but take the money and start a new life in America with your daughter. When you arrive there, I'll send you another 20,000 francs. Now get out. I never want to see you again!'

When Thénardier had left, unable to believe his good fortune, Marius ran to find Cosette and told her everything immediately.

'We must go to him at once,' Marius said. 'He was the man who saved my life. We must waste no time!'

Minutes later, he and Cosette were travelling in a carriage to Number 7, rue de l'Homme-Armé.

♦

Jean Valjean looked up when he heard the knock on his door and called in a weak voice, 'Come in.'

The door opened and Marius and Cosette appeared. Cosette rushed to the chair where Jean Valjean was sitting.

'Father!' she cried, falling into his arms.

'So you've forgiven me?' Valjean whispered, hugging Cosette to him and turning to Marius.

'Cosette, did you hear what he said?' Marius cried, tears of shame and guilt rolling down his cheeks. 'He asked *me* to forgive *him*. And do you know what he did? He saved my life and he brought me back to you. He came to the barricade to save me, just as he saved Javert. He carried me on his back through the sewers of Paris, to bring me to you. Oh Cosette, I feel so ashamed of the way I've treated him!'

'You have no need to say all this,' Valjean murmured.

'Why didn't you say it yourself?' Marius demanded. 'Why didn't you tell me that you were M. Madeleine and that you saved Javert's life at the barricade? Why didn't you tell me that I owed you my life?'

'Because I thought it would be better to break away. If you had known the truth, you would have felt obliged to be good to me, a worthless criminal. That would have upset everything.'

'What or whom would it have upset?' Marius said. 'Well, we're not going to allow you to stay here on your own. You're going to come home with us. You're Cosette's father and mine. I won't allow you to spend another day here.'

'And you can't refuse this time,' Cosette agreed, sitting on Jean Valjean's lap and kissing his forehead. 'There's a carriage waiting for you. I'm kidnapping you – by force, if necessary!'

Jean Valjean listened as she described the view from the room that would be his, the beauty of the garden, the singing of the birds, but he was listening more to the music of her voice than to the meaning of her words. Finally, he said, 'Yes, it would be delightful, but . . .'

Cosette, frightened, took his two hands in hers.

'Your hands are so cold,' she said. 'Are you ill? Are you in pain?'

'No,' said Valjean. 'I'm not in pain. But . . .'

'But what?'

'I'm going to die soon.'

'Father, no!' Cosette cried. 'You're going to live! You *must* live, do you understand?'

Marius and Cosette both did their best to raise Valjean's spirits, to show him how much they loved and needed him, to fill him with the strength and the desire to live again. But it was too late. Valjean smiled, his eyes shining with love and happiness, but he was beginning to lose strength.

'To die is nothing,' he murmured. 'But it is terrible not to live.'

Then, taking Cosette's sleeve and pressing it to his lips, he said, 'Come close to me, both of you. I love you dearly. How sweet it is to die like this. And you love me too, dear Cosette. You'll feel some grief for me, but not too much. I want you to have no great sorrows. You must enjoy life, my children. I'm leaving the two candlesticks by the bed to Cosette. They're made of silver, but to me they are pure gold. I don't know whether the person who gave them to me is pleased as he looks down on me from above. I've done my best. You mustn't forget, my children, that, despite my money, I am one of the poor.'

As he spoke, Valjean's breathing became more painful and he had difficulty moving his arms. But as the weakness of his body increased, his spirit grew in strength. The light of an unknown world was shining brightly in his eyes.

'Now, Cosette,' he breathed softly, 'the time has come for me to tell you your mother's name. It was Fantine. You must not forget it. Your mother loved you greatly and she suffered greatly. She was as rich in sorrow as you are in happiness. That is how God balances things out. He watches us all from above and knows what he is doing among his splendid stars. And now I must leave you, my children. Love one another always. There is nothing else that matters in this world except love.'

Cosette and Marius fell to their knees on either side of him, holding back their tears. Jean Valjean's hands rested on their bowed heads, and did not move again. He lay back with his head turned to the sky, the light from the two silver candlesticks falling on his smiling, peaceful face.

ACTIVITIES

Before you read

1 Think of five serious problems that poor people had 100 years ago. Compare your list with another student. Which of the problems you have chosen were the most serious, do you think? Which of these problems still exist today?

2 Find the words in *italics* in your dictionary. They are all in the story. Use them to complete the sentences below.

barber   casual   doll   franc   gaze   misery   murmur
prostitute   shiver   sigh

a She ..... with cold.
b He went to the .....'s to have his hair cut.
c She ..... at the picture.
d He ..... something to his friend.
e She played with her ......
f He ..... with impatience.
g She had no friends or money – she lived a life of ......
h She became a ......
i He changed his money into French ......
j It was a ..... meeting.

After you read

3 Which of the words below describe
   a Jean Valjean?   b the Bishop of Digne?   c neither?
   bitter   modest   dangerous   popular   desperate
   ashamed   confused

4 Put these sentences about Fantine in the correct order. Say why these things happen.
   a She is arrested.
   b She spits at a man.
   c She says goodbye to her daughter.
   d She goes to the barber's.
   e She goes to the dentist.
   f She loses her job.

99

g She feels happy.

h She becomes ill.

5 Discuss why M. Madeleine saves Champmathieu from prison. Is he right to do this, do you think? Why (not)?

Chapters 4–6

Before you read

6 How will Valjean react to Fantine's death, do you think? Why?

7 Find these words in your dictionary.

concierge   hug   mattress   slam   stockings   stove

Which is a word for

a a person who looks after a building?

b something you sleep on?

c something you wear?

d something that heats a room?

e an affectionate action?

f a noisy action?

After you read

8 Are these sentences true or false? Why?

a Mme Thénardier thinks the stranger is rich.

b Cosette slowly begins to trust the stranger.

c Apart from taking Cosette away, the stranger does three things to help Cosette.

d Thénardier thinks love is more important than money.

9 How do these people feel about each other, and why?

a M. Gillenormand and Georges Pontmercy

b Marius and Cosette

c Marius and Thénardier

d Marius and M. Gillenormand

10 Work in pairs and act out this imaginary conversation between Valjean and Cosette.

Student A: You are Valjean. You think that it is too dangerous to stay in the rue de l'Ouest. Explain why you must both leave, without telling her the truth about your past.

You are Cosette. You want to stay in the rue de l'Ouest. Try to persuade Valjean to change his mind about leaving. Don't tell him your true feelings about the young man in the Luxembourg Gardens.

Chapters 7–8

Before you read

11 What does Marius wish he had done differently in the Luxembourg Gardens, do you think? What would you do now, if you were Marius?

12 Answer the questions. Find the words in *italics* in your dictionary.
  a When was the last time you felt *despair*?
  b Do you enjoy *solitude*? Why (not)?

After you read

13 Who or what do the underlined words refer to?
  a <u>He</u> paid <u>their</u> rent.
  b <u>She</u> gives <u>him</u> a letter.
  c <u>His</u> business is cheating people out of money.
  d <u>She</u> offers to help <u>him</u>.
  e <u>He</u> pretends not to know <u>him</u>.
  f <u>He</u> doesn't know what to do.

14 Finish these sentences about Chapter 8.
  a Marius has less money than usual because ...
  b Éponine doesn't want Marius's money because ...
  c Cosette feels excited when she discovers ...
  d May 1832 is a happy month for Marius and Cosette because ...

Chapters 9–12

Before you read

15 At the end of the last chapter, Marius says, 'I'm going to try something.' What is he going to try, do you think? Why?

16 Find these words in your dictionary.
  aristocracy barricade blot cannon coffin stronghold
  Which words are connected with
  a fighting? b death? c power and wealth? d writing?

After you read

17 Choose the correct answer.

   a When he first sees his grandson, M. Gillenormand

      feels angry.

      hides his true feelings.

      makes him feel welcome.

   b Marius is angry with his grandfather because

      he's rude about his father.

      he insults Cosette.

      he refuses to give him any money.

18 In Chapter 10, who

    a wears a disguise?   **d** saves Marius's life?

    b is the rebels' leader?   **e** has been sent to spy on the

    c wants to die?   rebels?

19 How does Valjean discover that Cosette is in love?

Chapters 13–15

Before you read

20 Why has Valjean gone to the barricade? What is he going to do next, do you think?

21 Find these words in your dictionary.

   feast grille guardian obliged sewer wig

   Which words best complete the following phrases?

    a a blonde . . . . .   **d** a wedding . . . . .

    b to feel . . . . .   **e** looked after by a . . . . .

    c a metal . . . .   **f** an underground . . . . .

After you read

22 Discuss these questions with another student.

   a Why does Valjean tell Marius about his criminal past? What effect does this have?

   b What does he *not* tell Marius?

   c If you had been Valjean, would you have done the same? Why (not)?

23 With another student, act out this imaginary conversation between Marius and Cosette.

Student A: You are Marius. Tell Cosette why she must stop seeing Valjean.

Student B: You are Cosette. Tell Marius why you think he is wrong.

24 How does Marius discover the truth about Valjean?

Writing

25 Write a short story, saying what you think happened to Valjean after he stole the money from Petit-Gervais, and before his arrival in Montreuil as M. Madeleine two months later.

26 Imagine that you are a journalist. Write a report for your newspaper about the arrest of Thénardier and his friends (Chapter 7). Include an Interview with Inspector Javert.

27 Imagine that you are Éponine. Write a diary about your feelings for Marius. Describe your first meeting with him, and the events that bring you to the barricade in the rue de la Chanvrerie.

28 Choose one of the following subjects, and write about its importance to the story.

a letters   b false names   c Marius's father

29 Imagine that you are Inspector Javert. Write a letter to the police, to be found after your death. Explain your relationship with Jean Valjean, and why you decided to end your life.

30 Imagine that you are Cosette. You are upset because Valjean has stopped visiting you after your marriage to Marius. Write a letter to him, telling him how hurt you are and why you want to see him again.

Answers for the activities in this book are available from your local Pearson Education office or contact: Penguin Readers Marketing Department, Pearson Education, Edinburgh Gate, Harlow, Essex, CM20 2JE.

BESTSELLING
PENGUIN READERS

AT LEVEL 6

Brave New World

The Chamber

Cry, the Beloved Country

Great Expectations

Kolymsky Heights

Memoirs of a Geisha

Misery

Oliver Twist

Presumed Innocent

The Remains of the Day

Saving Private Ryan

Snow Falling on Cedars